The Addiction Process

From Enabling To Intervention

Helena Roche

Health Communications, Inc.
Deerfield Beach, Florida

Helena Roche, B. Soc. Sc., Dip. App. Soc. Stud.;
    C.Q.S.W.
Rutland Centre
Dublin, Ireland

Library of Congress Cataloging-in-Publication Data

Roche, Helena, 1950 —
    The addiction process: from enabling to intervention/Helena
Roche.
        p.   cm.
    ISBN 1-55874-005-8
    1. Alcoholics — Rehabilitation — United States.   2. Alco-
holics — United States — Family relationships.   3. Compulsive
behavior — Treatment — United States.   I. Title.
HV5279.R625   1989   88-24481
362.2'9—dc19   CIP

© 1990 Helena Roche
ISBN 1-55874-005-8

Publisher: Health Communications, Inc.
            3201 S.W. 15th Street
            Deerfield Beach, Florida 33442

Acknowledgments

I gratefully acknowledge the support of Rutland Centre management and staff in the preparation of this book. In particular, I thank Mr. Donal Glynn, M.A., Director of Rutland Centre for his continuing support.

The comments and guidance provided by Mr. John S. Baudhuin, of Glenbeigh Incorporated, Jupiter, Florida, were also deeply appreciated.

My sincere thanks to Noreen and Kevin Norris for their considerable help in the typing and assembling of the original manuscript.

Contents

Introduction vii

Part I   **What Is Enabling?** 1

Chapter 1   Enabling Awareness 3

Chapter 2   Control 11

Chapter 3   Protection 25

Chapter 4   Enabling Reversal 57

Part II   **Intervention** 77

Chapter 5   The Intervention Plan 79

Chapter 6   Implementing Intervention 165

Chapter 7   Format Of Intervention 181

Chapter 8   Intervention: Professionally
                   Facilitated 195

Chapter 9   Encounter With Reality 207

Chapter 10   Treatment 217

Chapter 11   Surprise Ending 239

References 245

Introduction

This book is intended to provide a basic explanation of alcohol, drug and gambling dependency. It particularly emphasizes the emotional and behavioral difficulties that develop gradually as the problem progresses. It aims to help you understand the needs and fears of a person whose drinking, drug-taking or gambling have become compulsive, rather than controlled. Armed with this knowledge you can begin intervention. This involves using strategies designed to help the person with the problem recognize and accept the need to seek professional help.

The book also should prove valuable on a personal basis. It offers explanation and support to help you cope effectively with emotional distress and to reverse patterns of behavior which no longer serve a useful function.

The rationale and process of intervention are considered in detail. Strategies are outlined, with a discussion of their values in contributing to initial recovery. Treatment and self-help groups are discussed as resources in the establishment of long-term sobriety.

A Note About Compulsive Gambling

Both alcohol and drug abuse involve the intake of mood-altering chemicals which have a direct effect on physical, emotional and behavioral functioning. Compulsive gambling does not involve chemical intake but, in every respect, it mimics the pathology of dependency. Research continues to establish the mechanisms which operate but current wisdom suggests that compulsive gambling involves marked alteration of mood with extreme *highs* and *lows*. It also gives rise to manipulation in order to secure funding and to defensiveness and protectiveness in relation to its use. The consequences of compulsive gambling are severe; financial and legal difficulties are common and family life is seriously disrupted. In 1980 the American Psychiatric Association delineated criteria for the diagnosis of compulsive gambling, thereby including it in the *Diagnostic and Statistical Manual* (DSM III) of the American Psychiatric Association.

Professionals working in the treatment field are familiar with the concept of *dual dependency*. Abuse of alcohol and gambling or abuse of alcohol and drugs are common combinations. For this reason, many centers offering professional treatment are drug-free and recommend complete abstinence from any mood-altering chemicals or experiences if recovery is to be attained and developed.

Recovery from dependency is possible with appropriate help. For many families the initial task is to contribute to successful intervention, so that the dependent person is offered the opportunity to get well and resume normal living. Family members and friends also experience positive benefits when they utilize treatment programs and self-support groups such as Al-Anon, Nar-Anon or Gamanon during the process of recovery.

Use Of Terms

For the sake of convenience, the person with the problem will be referred to as the dependent person, while relatives, friends or colleagues will be described as concerned persons.

To avoid repetitive and cumbersome use of "he" and "she," the dependent person will be referred to as "he" throughout. However, the text is equally applicable to a dependent person who is female.

PART
I

What Is Enabling?

1

Enabling Awareness

⬦ When a close friend or family member is in difficulty,
we have a natural tendency to help, if we can. Many
problems can be resolved by straightforward methods or by
the provision of emotional support during periods of adjustment. When faced with an alcohol, drug or gambling dependency, people tend to adopt a problem-solving focus in
an attempt to get things back to normal. Initially it seems
reasonable to concentrate on getting the dependent person
to stop excessive use. Family members and friends also try
to prevent or minimize the harmful consequences of alcohol, drug or gambling-related behavior. Usually a great deal
of effort is expended trying to achieve these goals. Concerned persons sometimes give up in disgust when their
well-intentioned efforts prove futile.

"I've tried everything, it's hopeless," they state angrily and
begin to concentrate, instead, on self-protection. Regretfully,
this may involve excluding the dependent person from their
lives. The real difficulty, of course, is that alcohol, drug and
gambling problems develop gradually, obliging others to re-

spond to their changing demands on a trial-and-error basis. Eventually family members find themselves locked into patterns of behavior which cannnot work effectively. We will examine the features of the developing illness and explore an alternative, effective approach to the problem — intervention.

What Is Addiction?

Addiction is an illness with recognizable symptoms. Physical dependency may develop — an indication that the user's body has become habituated to large quantities of alcohol or drugs. Health may be affected since certain types of bodily damage are associated with substance abuse. A medical evaluation is required to assess the extent of physical dependency or impaired health, although some individuals display the classic symptoms of dependency without experiencing any health problems. However, all dependent people are subject to certain emotional and behavioral changes. These create great difficulties for family members and friends as well as resulting in isolation and despair for the person with the problem.

Compulsion is a prominent feature, creating a desire to continue using alcohol, drugs or gambling despite subsequent damage to self and others. Defensiveness about the extent and implications of use is typical, making the dependent person increasingly unreachable. Memory lapses occur frequently with heavy-drinking or drug-taking so that the user cannot recall specific episodes.

Most dependencies eventually result in marked deterioration in personality and behavior patterns. The person's ability to maintain healthy relationships is damaged, as is his capacity to function effectively at work and within the community.

At present, let us underline that defensiveness, memory lapse and compulsion combine to ensure that the dependent person does not recognize the damage arising from alcohol, drug or gambling abuse. Lack of recognition of the problem on the part of the excessive user is, then, an important part of the illness. This is usually referred to as denial or self-delusion.

Concerned persons can unwittingly prolong the condition by becoming *enablers*. The term *enabling* is used to include any behavior by family members or friends which aims to contain or limit drinking, drug-taking or gambling or to shield the dependent person from the familial, legal, social or work-related implications of ongoing excessive use. Although based on a desire to resolve problems, enabling actually worsens a situation in the long term. It removes responsibility from the person whose drinking, drug-taking or gambling is creating difficulties. It, therefore, slows down his recognition of the illness which is developing and of the need to seek help.

Enabling can increase because family members and friends feel responsible for the dependent person. They interpret his disruptive behavior as an unwelcome reflection on themselves or as a threat to their competence and social standing. When working toward intervention, the notion of *responsibility for* is best translated into *responsibility toward* the troubled individual, who needs help of a specific type in order to get well. In recovery an excessive drinker, drug-taker or gambler will be encouraged to take personal responsibility for his dependency and to recognize sobriety as the only option for the future. Family members and friends can discharge their responsibilities by channeling energies in the direction of intervention and, later, by participating in the dependent person's treatment and recovery.

Continued enabling, however, makes recovery less likely. We will examine the range of behaviors that constitute enabling. Initially, we should recognize that family members and friends rarely intend to become enablers. In fact, most people are shocked when they eventually realize that their well-intentioned efforts have actually been prolonging the problem. The reasons for enabling can change over time as the dependency progresses in severity. Some family members or friends enable only to a limited extent or soon learn that enabling doesn't help. Others are constantly watchful and devote considerable time and energy to coping with the difficulties presented by the dependent person.

When recovery begins, some concerned persons reflect with astonishment on their years of enabling. Against all considerations of reason or logic, they engaged, repeatedly, in patterns of behavior detrimental to themselves and often contrary to their personal standards or values. At the time, of course, they saw their efforts as an attempt to counterbalance the disorder associated with the dependent person's behavior. They were also concerned to preserve normal standards within family life and to keep the troubled individual functioning optimally, at work and in society. They believed themselves to be acting in the best interests of everyone affected by the problem.

Enabling, Behavior And Attitude

Enabling involves both behavior and attitude. Preoccupation with control and protection can dominate the day-to-day life of family members to the point where normal activities are seriously disrupted and emotional growth is restricted. Enabling sometimes becomes the norm, indicating an unreflective, automatic response to each new demand presented by the dependency. As crises escalate, the perceived need to continue enabling maintains a dysfunctional dynamic within the family. Enabling, then, often acquires a momentum of its own. Reacting unthinkingly to each new crisis, concerned persons rely on old methods of response because their adaptability is reduced by continuing stress. The unrelenting demands of dependency create further reasons to enable. A pattern emerges which requires interruption. Education about enabling is a vital first step. With knowledge comes choice. Concerned persons can often give themselves permission to end enabling when they understand that it is fundamentally unhelpful. Nonenabling can feel uncaring until you understand its rationale. When the illness of dependency is fully accepted, it feels right not to enable further. Intervention becomes necessary and desire for recovery can replace concern for survival as the major motivator in a family.

Concerned persons enable because it initially seems the "right thing to do." It may now be helpful for us to examine some typical reasons for enabling.

Enabling Factors

Enabling can be based on one or several of the following factors:

1. A sense of loyalty to the dependent person.
2. A constructive desire to cope with the difficulties posed by the dependent person's behavior.
3. A sense of personal responsibility for creating or contributing to the alcohol, drug or gambling problem.
4. Public esteem — concern for the "good name" of the family.
5. Social concern — the desire to prevent damage to others when the dependent person is intoxicated.
6. The survival needs of the family unit.
7. A desire to prevent deterioration in the dependent person's social position or employability.
8. Fear of loss or damage to the relationship with the dependent person.
9. Fear for the dependent person's physical safety.
10. Fear of confronting an aggressive dependent person.
11. Pressure to stand by the dependent person from family members, friends or in-laws.
12. A desire to defer or avoid seeking outside help with the problem.
13. Lack of awareness of dependency as an illness on the part of those surrounding the troubled person.
14. An unrecognized personal desire to be needed by the dependent person.
15. An unrecognized personal desire to have power over the dependent person.

In understanding your own enabling it can be helpful to assess which considerations most influenced you as time went on. Some of the reasons outlined above are very valid. Occasionally, enabling is based mainly on personal need within the concerned person. Usually, however, it occurs because of a misconception about the nature of the problem or a misunderstanding of the type of help required by the dependent person.

Responsive Enabling

Often enabling is *responsive enabling*, a continuing re-action to the changing demands of the dependency over time. It is primarily motivated by the concerned person's desire to eliminate the alcohol, drug or gambling problem and minimize its disruptiveness within the family or work unit. Although considerable energy is devoted to enabling of this type, it usually is experienced as an unwelcome strain and eventually is resented by family members or friends. When concerned persons engaged in responsive enabling eventually learn that it prolongs the dependency, they often work hard to become nonenabling. They welcome the opportunity to "act" rather than "react" and respond positively to guidance about intervention strategies.

Invested Enabling

On the other hand, despite the need for an intervention-oriented approach, *invested enabling* is likely to be continued because it meets important personal needs of the enabler. For some concerned people the need to be needed is crucial. The troubled individual's growing preoccupation with alcohol, drugs or gambling makes him less self-reliant and increasingly dependent on others for care and protection. As he functions less effectively, the enabler feels needed and can find it difficult to adjust to the nonenabling approach that intervention requires. For others involved in invested enabling, the need to feel special is central. Dependent people feel increasingly misunderstood by others as the problem develops.

A concerned person who is repeatedly told, "You're the only one who understands me. I can always rely on you," may begin to find gratification in the role. It is then easy to discount or undermine the efforts of others when intervention is attempted. Occasionally a family member or friend has an unrecognized personal need to dominate. In such circumstances, the troubled individual's deteriorating ability to function effectively in important roles allows the enabler to feel superior and powerful. Invested enabling can also occur because of ambivalence about the future of the relationship. Intervention and recovery are perceived as threatening. They imply a process of change which is assumed to have implications of a long-term nature — "Perhaps he won't love me if he gets well." Concerned persons who are involved in invested enabling need considerable support in working toward intervention because they see recovery as a loss rather than a gain.

Let us now move on to describe enabling in more detail, so that you can become aware of the type of behavior usually included under this heading. It also is helpful to recognize the strain on both the individual and the family constant enabling requires.

What Is Enabling?

Enabling has two major elements.

Control

This includes:

1. *Monitoring* the dependent person's consumption or use.
2. *Contesting* the dominance of chemicals or gambling.

Protection

This includes:

1. *Denying* the problem to oneself.
2. *Concealing* the problem from others.
3. *Rationalizing* the implications of the problem.
4. *Correcting* the disorder arising from dependency.
5. *Compensating* for the dependent person's deterioration.
6. *Caretaking* of the dependent person.
7. *Supplementing* the dependent person's addictive supply.

Control

 Much enabling behavior is aimed at eliminating or restricting the abuse of alcohol, drugs or gambling on
the part of the dependent person.

Enabling aimed at control is based on the assumption that
the dependent person is freely choosing to misuse alcohol,
drugs or the gambling experience. It fails in the long-term
because the dependent person has a progressive illness which
gets worse over time. He is driven to continue the destructive
pattern of use in a compulsive way and is, therefore, out of
control. This type of enabling preoccupies concerned persons and allows the behavior of the dependent person to
dominate and shape the quality of the relationship. It leaves
family members and friends less free to take care of their
needs as individuals. It also requires constant vigilance and
reduces the energy available for normal activities.

Enabling aimed at controlling the problem inevitably fails.
This frustrates and disillusions those trying to control the
dependent person and produces feelings of anger, resentment
and contempt. These become directed at the troubled indi-

vidual. He, in turn, feels put upon, harassed and misunderstood and becomes increasingly resentful of other people's
interference with his drinking, drug-use or gambling. The
angry belief, "You're all against me," is common amongst
dependent people, whose first priority is to maintain supply.
Conflict results and eventually family members and friends
feel increasingly isolated from the troubled individual. They
begin to see him as uncaring, selfish and unconcerned with
appropriate standards of behavior as well as with other people's wishes and needs. Over time, this results in a weakening
of the emotional bond on which the relationship is built. As
mutual distrust and antagonism grow, concerned persons are
less able to use personal influence to encourage the troubled
individual to seek help. The more they control, the greater
the threat family members and friends pose to the dependent
person. Therefore, he is less likely to "hear" their concern for
him when it is expressed verbally.

Attempts to control the problem may include the following
behaviors by concerned persons.

Monitoring

Monitoring the dependent person's consumption is just one
way of trying to control the problem. When engaged in this
type of enabling, family members or friends take *direct
action*. They aim to prevent opportunities for drinking, drug-
taking or gambling or to limit the quantity of alcohol or
drugs consumed by the dependent person. In their response
to the problem some families experience phases during which
they focus considerable energy on this type of control. The
extent or type of monitoring which concerned persons undertake is affected by the pattern of use of the troubled
individual. A person who abuses alcohol, drugs or gambling
within the family home provides more opportunities for this
type of control than the absentee abuser.

Methods Of Control

- Attempting to control or withhold the dependent person's funds.

- Physically preventing the dependent person from getting to a source of supply.
- Disposing of unused alcohol or drugs.
- Accompanying the dependent person in order to monitor his consumption.
- Checking on the dependent person's movements.
- Avoiding normal social events and occasions at which drinking, drug-taking or gambling could occur.
- Requesting family members, friends or suppliers not to provide alcohol, drugs or opportunities for gambling.

Effects Of Control On The Individual

There are various ways that the troubled individual can be affected by the monitoring of his problem.

- Creating antagonism and defiance toward those who represent a threat to supply.
- Providing a built-in rationalization for continuing abuse. "Nobody is going to treat me like that." "Why shouldn't I drink, since I'm unhappy at home?"
- Increasing the likelihood of quarreling and physical aggression.
- Fostering manipulation by the dependent person in securing, concealing and protecting supply.
- Slowing down the dependent person's recognition of his personal loss of control.
- Encouraging avoidance of family members or friends who have a genuine concern for the dependent person's well-being.
- Fostering increased involvement with heavy drinkers, drug-takers or gamblers.

Effects Of Control On Those Around

These are various ways that concerned persons can be affected by the monitoring of the troubled individual's problem.

- Absorbing a disproportionate level of energy and time resulting in neglect of constructive activities and emotional needs.

- Dominating the consciousness of family members, occasionally to the point of obsession.
- Focusing on the specifics of drinking, drug-taking or gambling, thereby preventing recognition of other emerging symptoms of dependency.
- Contributing to a family perception of the dependent person as selfish, untrustworthy or bad because he refuses to cooperate.
- Generating anger, resentment and anxiety in those involved.
- Fostering countermanipulation and game-playing within the family unit.
- Engaging children in the conflict between partners and creating a tense family atmosphere in which self-expression is restricted.
- Disrupting social life, due to self-imposed avoidance, or the involvement of friends in the monitoring process.

A Perfect Team

My father was a drinker and my mother an anti-drinker. We five children were vigilantes. Lots of families have a private language, catchphrases, shared jokes that mean little to outsiders. We were no exception. If all five of us were ever, for some reason, to raise our voices in unison we'd chant, "Find the bottle." For years we operated as spies on constant seek-and-destroy missions. My father never had enough to drink. He got the shakes in the morning and needed a "cure." He always brought a bottle home no matter how late it was. We older children would be waiting up. We all had preassigned roles. One of us would search the car, another the garden shrubbery. If it wasn't too late, one of the younger kids would be sent to sit on his lap and figure out which pocket the bottle was in. Then, target located, we'd wait. He'd fall asleep eventually and the *Panthers* would move into action. Bottle secured, Mother poured the alcohol down the drain. Then we went to bed to catch a few.hours sleep before he woke up, roaring, "Where's my whiskey? Who took it?"

Mother, of course, could never resist letting him know just what she thought of him. There were terrible rows, sometimes coming to blows. Sick with fear, we'd lie and listen, wanting to protect Mother but afraid of our father. I often covered my head with a pillow, cursing myself for the coward I was but blaming my mother for starting the argument.

But Dad wasn't stupid either. After a while he'd bring home two or three bottles and hide them in ingenious locations. We'd usually find one, possibly two. He was nearly always sure of his morning "cure" — if he could remember where he'd hidden it.

Then my mother decided he couldn't drink if he had no money. She was organized about it. She'd like to have had his paycheck paid directly to her but was afraid he'd lose the job if she told Dad's employers about him. But she took whatever money he had left at night and hoarded it away. How clearly I remember those mornings. My father banging around upstairs, flinging the content of drawers and wardrobes on the floor, looking for his cash. Eventually he'd come downstairs with blazing eyes and refuse to let any of us go to school until we told him where it was. My mother wouldn't want to give in. She could be quite implacable. But we were so tense and already late for the bus that we'd end up pleading with her. Sometimes she gave it and sometimes she didn't. My father hated her and called her names.

I'll never forget the venom between them at those times. Our house was a battlefield. The atmosphere of tension was unbearable. My father was always yelling, "You're all against me!" I suppose we were. He felt he had to fight us all the time so we never saw him in any other mood. He'd get maudlin sometimes but that was just alcohol.

He and my mother never went out together. She flatly refused to drink with him and he wasn't interested in doing anything else. She had all her friends alerted. "Don't, under any circumstances, offer Tom a drink." Of course it meant she couldn't go visiting with him either, say to a party or something, in case there'd be alcohol there.

Everything was centered on the family. Dad's drinking was the problem and he had to be made to stop. Perhaps our motto should have been *"Abstinence makes the heart grow fonder"* because, while he drank, there was no love. We kids were all caught up in it. Mother approved of us if we managed to outwit Dad. If we didn't, her anger surfaced and we suffered. If we did the slightest thing wrong, we'd "Drive Dad to drink." Eventually I disliked Mother as much as Father. I felt she provoked and aggravated. Once, in a bout of sarcasm, I suggested we move to an alcohol-free state. I was miserable. We were all miserable.

I remember getting up one morning to go to the bathroom. I opened the door and was almost inside when I realized my father was there. He was hanging over the sink, vomiting and crying. He had the water running to hide the sounds. He was sobbing as though his heart would break. I felt a lump in my throat and my eyes filled with tears. For the first time in years, I really saw him. He looked sick and old and despairing. I tried to say "Dad" but my voice didn't work. I wanted to touch him — to help him. I don't know what would have happened but right at that moment my mother passed by. I remembered where my loyalties lay. I closed the door again and went straight to school without waiting for breakfast. That night he was drunker than ever . . .

Contesting

Contesting the dominance of chemicals or gambling is another way of controlling the problem.

Close human relationships imply reciprocated or complementary need between parties. They also involve acceptance of and by the other, together with an element of mutual influence. Role-based involvements include mutual obligations and commitments to agreed codes of behavior. These structure the expectations and interchanges between participants to varying extents. Viable relationships require continuing investment by those involved.

When dependency is developing, the troubled individual is so preoccupied with alcohol, drug or gambling abuse that he invests less time and energy in important relationships. Others perceive this as hurtful and threatening. They respond by trying to force the required commitment from the dependent person. The reasoning is simple, at this time — "Drinking, drug-taking or gambling is interfering with our life together. If this is eliminated, we'll be back to normal." Family members or friends begin to utilize the same tactics the person with the problem appears to employ. "If you can withdraw, so can I," "If you won't live up to your obligations, I'll punish you." By personal appeal, limit-testing, condition-setting and retaliation, concerned persons aim to control the troubled individual's behavior by stopping his drinking, drug-taking or gambling.

While the positions adopted are superficially similar, there is a major difference between the motivation of concerned and dependent persons at this time. The troubled individual usually invests less, due to the compulsion associated with dependency. His failure to participate is not so much a choice as a telling indication of the extent to which chemicals have acquired priority in his day-to-day life. Concerned persons are motivated by fear and anger. Their sense of indignation is strong. So is the belief that strategies must be found to force the troubled person to reinvolve himself in the relationship in the old way. It becomes a contest for primacy, for first place: a win-lose situation, in which the relationship itself is placed on the line.

"Prove you love me more than alcohol/drugs/gambling." In such circumstances, family members or friends operate on the mistaken assumption that the person with the problem retains control and can, therefore, choose to stop. Ironically, they become caught up in the same battle with chemicals which the dependent person is waging. They, too, want to beat it, they, too, believe they can *win*.

Chemical dependency and compulsive gambling have all the characteristics of addiction. To restore normality, the troubled individual must stop their use. To become able to do this successfully he needs outside help. When the family engages in the win-lose battle, it assumes the problem can be resolved by some shift in balance within the relationship or family unit. What is actually needed, of course, is specialist help to place the problem in the context in which it belongs — addiction: an illness from which recovery is possible with appropriate help.

Enabling, based on contesting, creates considerable disorder within a family. It inevitably generates conflict, disillusionment and resentment. It also brings failure — diminished self-esteem within family members and apathy concerning the future of the relationship. While the win-lose battle is at its height, concerned persons suffer extreme distress. They experience rage, sadness, guilt and fear, all of which are raw and painful emotions. People feel rejected and want to retaliate. They are frightened and want to feel safe again. They are often stunned by the maelstrom of powerful emotions which accompany any conflict with the dependent person. They, too, feel out of control.

For many family members and friends, the emotional pain becomes unbearable. It can result in acts of desperation or the adoption of a sick identity. "I'm depressed; I can't cope." More usually, though, people detach themselves. To maintain stability they bury emotions and lose the ability to care. "You can do what you like, I couldn't care less." In the end, defeat is admitted but the price tag is high — years of family conflict, emotionally distressed children and un-healed emotional scars.

Contesting the dependency obscures the family problem and its solution by making the relationship itself the channel of conflict. What is needed is understanding of dependency and education about intervention and recovery. This is the only tactic which can possibly work. Early introduction to a new way of thinking can prevent years of misery and bitterness. A nonenabling approach preserves the best of the relationship and accelerates recovery and rebuilding of the family unit.

There are various contesting behaviors used by family members or friends. They include strategies to test limits, set conditions, retaliate or sanction the dependent person's behavior. They are applied on an *ad hoc* basis, to prevent or respond to the repeated occurrence of drinking, drug-taking or gambling. Their use is motivated by emotion and excessive reactions occur frequently.

Examples Of Contesting Behavior

- Persuading or humoring the dependent person in an attempt to avoid drinking, drug-taking or gambling episodes.
- Exhorting the dependent person to change his beverage or limit his intake.
- Pleading or begging and extraction of promises — "If you loved me, you wouldn't."

- Using a sexual relationship manipulatively to approve or punish.
- Nagging or silent treatment employed as method of control.
- Threatening separation or other sanctions without follow-through.
- Confronting angrily or threatening at a time when the troubled individual is unreceptive which increases his defensiveness.

Effects On The Individual

Contesting behaviors on the part of concerned persons can have various effects on the individual with the problem.

- Creation of guilt on a temporary basis but erratic, over-dramatic behavior of others can quickly be discounted as exaggerated.
- Avoiding rationalization for the dependent person's avoidance of commitments and his absenteeism from family life, as well as justification for his continual preoccupation with alcohol, drugs or gambling. "I can't face another evening listening to your nagging! I'm going out," or "Of course I drink. My wife doesn't understand me."
- Fostering manipulation of the emotions of others, on the part of the dependent person, that is persuading, cajoling, buying time, blaming and attacking or even the formation of alliances with sympathetic family members and friends.
- Extracting promises only encourages the dependent person's belief that he intends to stop someday. The presence of the intention absolves him from commitment to take the steps that would help him achieve recovery.
- Increasing the likelihood of oblivion-seeking alcohol, drug or gambling abuse because of the conflict and aftermath associated with individual episodes.
- Producing resentment, counterattacks and retaliatory attitudes toward others, who are perceived as the enemy.

- Negating the impact of a serious use of sanctions. Empty threats engender a false sense of security. Consequences can be discounted, since there is no follow through.

Effects On Those Around

Enabling, based on contesting, can affect concerned persons in various ways.

- Reinforcing feelings of rage, hatred and resentment when personal appeals are rejected by the dependent person.
- Generating tension, despair and depression.
- Creation of instability in the family due to erratic, unpredictable behavior.
- Concerned persons becoming targets for attack, disparagement and undermining as the person with the problem becomes more self-protective.
- Labeling of a family member as hostile, unstable or depressed, thereby enabling the dependent persons or others not to take them seriously with respect to the drinking, drug-taking or gambling.
- Fostering the emergence of cliques, sub-groups and exclusive alliances, as family members and friends take up positions in relation to the conflict.
- Leading to diminished self-esteem — failure to control the dependent person by the power of the relationship is internalized as inadequacy by family members or friends. "I'm not important. I don't count."
- Fostering the marital conflict myth between partners and in others, so that excessive drinking, drug-taking or gambling becomes viewed as a symptom of unhappiness, rather than a problem in itself.

Obsessed

I loved Ron when I married him. It was one of those fairy tale romances and I really believed we'd live happily ever after. How naive I was. Naturally, I wanted to stay at home and have a family.

We had two adorable children in rapid succession. I felt wonderful. My mother helped me a lot and I really enjoyed being with the children when they were young. I was happy. I felt I had it all, the good life and a handsome husband. He was working pretty hard at that time but I knew enough about business to realize that he had to put in long hours. He was often exhausted when he came home and liked to have a few drinks to relax. I thought nothing of it. In fact, I rather liked that part of the day. The children were in bed, we could talk a bit and catch up on each other's news.

I don't think I really noticed that he was beginning to drink too much. Some evenings he wouldn't come home because of a business meeting. He'd say he was eating out and not to wait up for him. I was disappointed, naturally, but lots of wives were in my position. I had the house, the children, my friends.

After a few years, I began to get a bit irritated with him. He was tired all the time and often out late. He said it was the pressure of work. I believed him but felt it was unfair. I began to wonder if it was me? Perhaps I wasn't attracting him any more? We hardly ever made love and I felt distant from him. He never wanted to talk any more and was irritable when I'd tell him about the children's day. He lost his temper with them a few times. I was appalled. I began to get angry with him and even accused him of not loving us. The atmosphere at home became tense.

I wondered if he had another woman and went through a phase of trying to attract him. I'd dress up, put on makeup and wait . . . wait. His hours became more and more erratic and when he did come home, he always smelled of alcohol.

I began to wonder just how much he was drinking. I started checking bottles in the drinks cupboard. I surprised him one night in the kitchen. He was drinking vodka and had almost finished a full bottle. I really lost my temper then. I accused him of wasting money, being half-drunk all the time. He just pushed me away and I started to cry. I begged him to tell me what was wrong with me. Didn't he like me any more? Didn't he want to talk to me any more? Had he stopped loving me? He told me not to be ridiculous and to go to bed. He said he was tired of my nagging and if he wanted to have a drink, he was entitled to. Wasn't he the one keeping the whole show on the road?

I really began to think after that. So drinking was important to him. I was very disappointed. I felt it was weak of him to need to drink in order to do his job and take care of his family. Yet I was sorry for him. He wasn't quite my idol anymore but I was determined to save him from himself. I assumed he'd fallen in with a hard-drinking crowd at work and he needed more home-life and healthy relaxation. I began to plan. I'd plead, persuade, cajole and seduce him into spending time with us. I told him the children needed him; I needed him. I'd cry and weep and give him the cold shoulder. I even threatened to leave him. I didn't really mean it. I just thought it would frighten him into taking me seriously.

He grew more and more impatient and annoyed with me. He used to tell me to get off his back. I accused him of trying to recapture his bachelor days and of evading his responsibilities. I told him I hated him. He got really angry then and attacked me verbally. He told me I was a nag, was boring in bed, that I'd used him to get a house and children and that I didn't care about him at all. I was shocked. I pleaded with him. I told him over and over again how much I loved him, needed him, wanted him home. Why couldn't he just do this for me? What did his drinking buddies have that I didn't have? I remember the contempt in his eyes as he looked at me, tears running down my face, the mascara I'd so carefully applied earlier streaking my cheeks.

"You're disgusting," he said. "No wonder I can't stand being with you." And then he walked out. He stayed away a whole weekend. I was frantic. I spent all the time crying, holding the children and weeping. They were terrified. All I could think of was revenge. "I'll make him pay. I'll get him back."

From then on, I began to act two parts, one the voluptuous seductress who made a point of flirting with other men when we were out. I'd watch him out of the corner of my eye, hoping to make him jealous. Most of the time, he hardly even noticed. He was drunk.

My other role was martyred little mother. I spent entire days crying and when he came home at night, I was waiting. I never went to bed before him. I told him I couldn't sleep when he wasn't there. Really looking back, I just wanted to make him feel bad. I complained all the time. I criticized him constantly to my mother and, I'm sorry to say, to the children. I felt he was nasty, uncaring and selfish.

The more I begged, nagged and cried, the more angry he was with me. When I complained about his drinking, he said I was driving him to it. One night we had a real row about that. So I said, "Fine! I'll stop nagging if you stop drinking." He said he'd try. I was full of hope. I began to dress nicely at home again, cook his favorite foods, plan family outings with the children. I even bought a sex manual, to try to improve my technique. He didn't drink for ten days but he was impossible to live with. He was irritable and short-tempered. I often gritted my teeth to keep my own temper under control. I suggested we see a marriage counselor in order to work things out. He refused point-blank and stormed out of the house, saying there was nothing wrong with him. That night, he was drunk again.

This time, I really let go. I screamed and raved and threatened. I even threw a shoe at him. The children woke up, frantic. Our oldest son tried to separate us. It was dreadful. I felt so bad the next day. But I was angry, so very angry with him. I hated him and I felt he was ruining our lives.

Then I began to drop out of things. I was too apathetic to go out with my friends. I'd spend the day in a dressing gown, slouching around the house. I felt he didn't love me. I was miserable all the time, full of self-pity.

He kept drinking. His hours grew more erratic and he began to stay out all night. That's when I really began to believe he was seeing another woman. I often followed him to check where he was. I discovered his favorite bar. Whenever I could get a babysitter, I'd spend hours outside, waiting to see who he was with. I'd sit there crying, feeling my world was falling apart. I hated him but I didn't want to lose him. I had no idea how to get him back. People had begun to tell me I'd changed, my mother in particular. She was right, I think. I used to be happy, cheerful, constructive. Now, I felt I was nothing. If my husband didn't love me, if he wouldn't stop drinking and pay attention to me, then how could I like myself? He was the center of my world.

3

Protection

To ensure that the well-being of the family unit is not threatened by excessive drinking, drug-taking or gambling, many concerned persons avoid being open about the extent of the problem. They also are motivated by loyalty in concealing the dependent person's difficulties from others. Considerable effort is expended trying to neutralize or deflect the consequences of uncontrolled behavior. The troubled individual is protected from sanctions imposed within the family and friendship network as well as by society. *In particular, concerned persons try to prevent any loss of social standing or employability as a result of his excessive drinking, drug-taking or gambling.*

A small proportion of vulnerable concerned persons try to change their personality or behavior patterns in an attempt to meet the demands or apparent needs of the troubled individual. In doing so, they assume responsibility for the problem, believing they are personally inadequate in some way. Quite often, this belief is reinforced by hostile comments or blaming on the part of the dependent person. In general such family members or friends feel badly about themselves inside. They often are socially isolated with few sources of positive input. For these reasons, securing the approval of the dependent person seems crucial. Unfortunately the effort involved in revamping is considerable and this emotionally costly effort to please has no lasting impact. Then confusion and disillusionment follow, with the concerned persons feeling cheated, rejected and inadequate.

Mood Mirroring

In other families the moods of the troubled individual dominate the household. When he is gloomy, depressed or angry, others feel unable to remain cheerful or to maintain a sense of well-being. On the other hand, when a spouse or family member is sad or anxious about a genuine difficulty, the dependent person may become impatient if his own current good mood is not matched by others. This process can be called *mood-mirroring* and often indicates a growing unwillingness to regard family members as separate individuals, each with a right to their own emotions. Eventually those surrounding the dependent person begin to avoid spontaneous expressions of emotion in his presence. Therefore, the person with the problem may gradually acquire the false belief that his needs are more important than those of other household members. Mood-mirroring can frustrate relatives and friends and contribute to self-absorption in the troubled individual.

Since the dependent person is out of control and likely to behave irresponsibly, there are frequent crises arising from alcohol, drug-taking or gambling-related activities. To protect the security of the family or the troubled individual, relatives or friends may take charge and assume full responsibility for resolving the difficulties. They also may begin to take over the functions of the dependent person, who is seen as unable or unwilling to cope.

These role changes usually create a sense of exclusion in the person with the problem. With the passage of time, he begins to feel increasingly valueless and undermined within the family. Enabling of this type also has the effect of reducing the dependent person's tolerance for stress, making him increasingly unable to face his problems directly. The troubled individual, therefore, learns little about the severity of his alcohol, drug or gambling problem as long as the impact of associated crises continues to be diminished by the protective response of others.

Enabling based on protection, then, allows the dependent person to avoid the anxiety arising from disruptive behavior and unfulfilled responsibilities. In particular, it allows him to maintain the delusion that there is no problem. It also prolongs the dependency by delaying a serious personal evaluation of the impact of excessive drinking, drug-taking or gambling, both on oneself and others. To protect the problem person, family members also overburden themselves by assuming additional roles and responsibilities. They feel forced to engage in manipulative behavior on his behalf, which can damage self-esteem and generate unease. In addition, the ongoing strain of avoiding openness about the problem can result in loss of supportive social contacts and restriction of normal activities.

The above factors give rise to anger with the dependent person, followed by a sense of deep disappointment at his inadequacy and continuing reckless behavior. People begin to expect less of the troubled individual and assume he is incapable of functioning normally. He may gradually lose respect as partner, parent, friend or employee in the eyes of family members and friends. This categorizes him as inadequate, infantile, dependent and further reduces his self-esteem. It also increases the concerned person's sense of being alone and unsupported in coping with daily life.

Types Of Protection-Based Enabling

Denying The Problem To Oneself

Some concerned persons experience great difficulty facing the implications of dependency. Threatened and fearful, their strongest impulse is to avoid thinking about the problem. Anxiety and uncertainty are defused by denial. By pretending to oneself that nothing is wrong, security and peace of mind are preserved. Denial is an understandable, and often useful, response to life situations which threaten us. By employing this mechanism we temporarily cushion ourselves against the impact of stress. We gain time and a breathing space before the problem is faced. Eventually, though, an emotionally healthy person will deal with the issue, however unpleasant. Then reality is accepted and a process of coping is initiated.

In the case of dependency, concerned persons often employ denial as a self-protective mechanism. It is particularly likely to be used in the early phase as the problem begins to develop. Family members or friends may avoid facing the implications of excessive drinking, drug-taking or gambling for as long as possible. When forced to confront it, they minimize its significance and hope the problem will resolve itself without the necessity for action. Denial of this type usually is short-term. Reality intrudes as the dependency worsens. Eventually those concerned acknowledge that steps must be taken. With information and support an intervention process can begin.

Key figures in the dependent person's life occasionally persist in the use of denial on a long-term basis. They avoid the problem completely by pretending it doesn't exist. Those living with dependency can be severely stressed by messages of denial given by others. For example, the parents of a person with a developing problem can feel unsupportive and threatened when the spouse expresses anxiety about alcohol, drug or gambling abuse. Their inclination is to rationalize and defuse anxiety. "It can't be as serious as you say. Could you be exaggerating? Perhaps it's just a phase, pressure of work? Let's wait and see."

If influential members of a dependent person's family or friendship network employ denial in a persistent way, they increase the burden carried by those attempting intervention. Their nonacceptance of the facts creates conflict. Those who want the problem acknowledged as real are forced to justify their plans to seek help. In addition, emphatic denial-based statements by family members or friends, who are avoiding the issue, make others doubt their evaluation of the seriousness of the problem. As a consequence, essential help-seeking responses are postponed and the dependency continues uninterrupted.

In summary, denial of the developing alcohol, drug or gambling problem is common. Those directly affected on a day-to-day basis may employ denial to protect themselves from anxiety and threat. Furthermore, a concerned person who wants to face the issue openly can feel hampered and unsupported by the denial of others.

A Nonconversation

Susan:

Mom, I really need to talk to you. Have you time? I'm very worried about Jenny. She's taking drugs and I think she needs help. I saw her two days ago, met her by chance in the street. You know she doesn't want to see me anymore. She's cut me out of her life. I'm not even sure where she's living now. I called round at her apartment and was told she'd moved out. There was this fellow there. He wasn't helpful at all. He was annoyed. He said she'd fallen behind with her rent and had been evicted. When I asked where she was now, he vaguely said he thought she was crashing with someone. I got really worried and went to her job. She wasn't in that day. Her supervisor was glad to see me. He said there was a problem. She's been missing work, looks sloppy all the time, can't seem to concentrate. He asked me if anything was wrong. I said I wasn't sure but promised I'd try to find out. He told me he thought she was abusing drugs. Her colleagues had noticed and the company was concerned for her job. He said they could help with her rehabilitation, but first she needs to be made to see the problem. It's called *intervention.* The company has a counselor. They'll help. They just need us, her family, to cooperate. That's what I wanted to talk to you about, Mom. Could you come along with me to meet this counselor? Maybe then we can decide what to do.

Mother:

Susan, I'm amazed at you. How can you talk that way about your sister? How could you go to her place of work and discuss her with a supervisor? Think of the damage you've done to her position there. How could you be so unthinking? I can't believe this. But, then, you were always jealous of Jenny. She was the bright one — got a good job.

I really believe you just want to hurt her. And as for this talk of drugs. What nonsense! Perhaps she doesn't want to see *you* but she came to see *me* here last week. She looked fine. She said things were wonderful, that she was due for promotion at work. She looked nice, neat, maybe a little thin but . . . I did notice she had shadows under her eyes and she was pale. I thought perhaps she wasn't taking good care of her health and eating properly but she just said she was working very hard on an important project and was due a vacation soon. She told me not to worry about her. She was just fine, Susan. I can't understand why you're making such a fuss. All these terrible accusations. Counselor indeed! Under no circumstances will I go to see a counselor and you certainly shouldn't go back there again. I'm sure, if she missed work, it's because of this special project. You probably just talked to somebody who didn't understand the important work she does. Really, Susan, how could you do this?

Susan:

But Mom, it's serious! You know Jenny always wanted you to think well of her. She probably put on a good face when she visited. When I met her in the street the other day, she looked anything but neat. She was actually dirty. Her hair was unwashed, her clothes were grubby and she was with some fellow who looked just the same as she did. She could hardly talk to me. Her words were slurred, her eyes were out of focus. I saw a bottle of pills in her purse. She was wearing a kaftan with loose sleeves. There were track marks on her arm, Mom. Don't you realize what that means? She's mainlining! Mom, we have to do something. She could die! Please, Mom, Jenny always listened to you. Won't you help?

Mother:

I really don't want to discuss this any further, Susan. You're absolutely wrong. If Jenny is overtired and taking a few pills to relax, I'll give her some money to have a nice vacation. She'll be fine then. Now I must go. I've arranged to go out to lunch and I don't want to be late. Drop in again sometime.

Concealing The Problem From Others

Most concerned persons affected by an alcohol, drug or gambling dependency conceal the abuse from others to some extent. This is understandable, particularly in the case of acquaintances. Motives vary considerably. Some people feel threatened by the implications of disclosure, fearing a catastrophe such as job loss. Covering-up with employers is common (although many companies have Employee Assistance Programs with the option of treatment for active dependency).

Some family members regard the troubled individual's excessive drinking, drug-taking or gambling as an unpleasant reflection on themselves. Their assumption is that, "If I disclose how things are in the family, people will think there is something wrong with me." In other circumstances, the dependent person demands secrecy and can place his family or friends under a great deal of pressure to conceal the problem. More usually spouse or children choose to hide the excessive use as a gesture of loyalty to the troubled individual.

Concealing the problem from immediate family members or close friends unfortunately carries the penalty of isolation for concerned persons. To maintain secrecy, they feel obliged to lie to and manipulate important people in their lives. Evasion and avoidance become habitual responses when questions are asked. Soon honest communication is impossible as guilt and tension increase. The enabling person feels restricted and isolated as the web of deceit becomes more and more burdensome. Outsiders are a threat and are assumed to be judgmental. Concealment forces the family to utilize its own resources to resolve the problem. Unfortunately, without information and guidance, most concerned persons enable rather than work toward long-term resolution of the difficulty. Oddly enough, people not directly affected by the problem can sometimes see the issue quite clearly — abuse of alcohol, drugs or gambling. They are less hampered by uncertainty and ambivalence than concerned persons who are closely involved. Occasionally, an outsider can make an unbiased evaluation of the nature of the difficulty and suggest a helpful course of action. By excluding others family members or friends limit their resources when affected by dependency. If unsupported and frightened, it is easy to lose perspective and avoid seeking help. Enabling, based on concealing, may include the following behavior by concerned persons.

Examples Of Concealing

- Avoiding or lying to employers, relatives or friends about the existence or extent of the problem.
- Instructing family members not to discuss the addicted person's behavior with outsiders, thereby restricting their access to support and creating a family secret.
- Providing excuses or socially acceptable explanations to deflect or mislead others, who have noticed the dependent person's excessive use of alcohol, drugs or gambling.

This type of enabling may have the following effects on the dependent person:

- It reinforces rationalization to protect self-esteem. "I'm all right. Other people see me as an okay fellow."
- It allows the self-delusion of dependency to become firmly established because a facade of normality is maintained with outsiders.
- It contributes to the street angel/house devil syndrome, as the immediate family becomes the only safe outlet for growing tension and frustration.

Enabling of this type may have the following effects on concerned persons:

- It increases social isolation, creating tension and stress during social encounters.
- It obliges family members or friends to engage in manipulative behavior contrary to their standards of conduct.
- It alienates those who suspect a problem and cues them to avoid sensitive topics.
- Reduced social or emotional accessibility to others decreases the likelihood of an intervention attempt originating from outside the family.

A Shadowed Childhood

Nobody ever discussed my father's drinking. I wasn't supposed to talk about it. My mother never said that to me but I knew. It was a secret. Even my Aunt Jane didn't know and I spent a lot of time with her when I was young. It was hard not to be able to tell someone. I was really ashamed. I never mentioned my father to my friends at school and if I ever brought them home, I made sure they came at a time when I knew he was working late. I didn't want them to meet him. I was afraid he'd be drunk. I never directly lied but I know some of my friends thought my father was dead. They were polite and didn't ask questions. I was grateful.

I can remember the sense of shame, even today. I felt so sorry for my mother but kind of angry with her, too. She always put a brave front on things. She went to work to earn money — long, hard hours as a waitress. She bought my school uniforms, my clothes, gave me my pocket money. I was an only child and I felt I had to be good, to make it up to her in some way. She was very loving toward me and she never complained about my father. She was proud, too proud to admit he was drinking, even to her sister. It was a conspiracy of silence — like a net. I watched everything I said when I was with people. I believed they'd laugh or feel contempt or pity us if they knew. I felt so lonely. But I couldn't tell anyone, not even my mother. She was so good to me and I didn't want to hurt her by being unhappy.

Rationalizing To Oneself And To Others

It is easy to rationalize our own mistakes and those of the people to whom we are close. Rationalizations are often presented as explanations. "This is how it happened. I was . . ." We can also avoid remorse or embarrassment by providing ourselves with acceptable excuses for our conduct. "I couldn't help it because . . ." Rationalizations make it easier to retain the good opinion of others and to protect our self-esteem.

When excessive drinking, drug-taking or gambling become obvious in the daily life of the dependent person, it is normal for family members and friends to rationalize. They feel loyal to the person with the growing problem and try to present his behavior in the best possible light. They use rationalization in a subtle way, to imply that each episode is isolated and explicable. "Sorry Joe drank a little too much at your house last night. He had a bad week at work and was letting his hair down." Explanations of this kind are intended to deflect attention from the problem. They also provide an acceptable cause.

Examples Of Rationalization

- Explaining the dependent person's disruptive behavior in terms intended to lessen its impact and make it excusable, i.e., labeling him as shy, sensitive, troubled, in poor health, under pressure at work or married to the wrong person.
- Overemphasizing the good qualities of the person with the problem to divert the attention of others from the unpleasant behavior associated with dependency: "Very intelligent/generous/hardworking person."
- Avoiding the current problem by dwelling on the past or living for the future. "We had wonderful times together in the early days. If only it could be like that again" or "Things will be better when he's older/gets married/gets promotion/retires."
- Wiping the slate clean, by accepting the dependent person's promises to stop without help or by being unduly optimistic about short-term improvements: "Well, okay then, I'll give you one more chance." "Perhaps he doesn't need help. He can stop when he wants to."
- Failing to use one's personal influence or role in the dependent person's life to encourage him to seek outside help. "There's nothing further I can do," "He won't listen to me. I don't count."

Rationalizing to oneself and to others can have the following effects on the dependent person:

- It obscures the growing dependency by creating an alternative labeling process: sick, tired, overworked, which is more socially and personally acceptable to the troubled individual than drunk, drug-dependent, etc.

- The search for causes increases the likelihood of inappropriate, help-seeking behavior, i.e. consultation for nervous tension, anxiety or depression. Medications prescribed are usually abused, possibly giving rise to dual dependency.
- It protects the troubled individual from realistic confrontation by influential people in his life, i.e. colleagues, employers, parents, siblings.

Rationalizing to oneself and others can have the following effects on concerned persons:

- It confuses concerned outsiders by forcing confrontation rather than discussion if they want to make comment on the dependent person's problem.
- The assumption of an underlying cause assumes a solution can be achieved by the employment of tactics or maneuvers to get the troubled individual to stop.
- It isolates immediate family members and friends from potential support because rationalizations appear to dismiss the concern of those who hear them. The underlying message is, "There's no need to be worried. Things are under control," or "You're intruding. Please mind your own business."
- It obscures the basic problem for concerned persons since they, too, accept rationalizations as real explanations. "He'd be fine if it wasn't for his job. Perhaps he needs a change."

Of Nervous Disposition

Harry:
Look, Louise, I know you're worried about Sharon. We all are. She really hasn't been well since she had the hysterectomy. Kind of depressed, you know. Just can't seem to bounce back. The doctor says she's physically recovered but otherwise . . . so so. She sleeps a lot, stays in bed during the day. I suppose she's just depressed. She's under the care of a psychiatrist now. He's got her on some anti-depressant. I'm sure they'll help. Time, really, is what's needed. Time and concern. She can't be put under any pressure, you know. We try to protect her, avoid worrying her.

We're doing all we can. I appreciate your concern, Louise, but things will work out.

Louise:

Well, Harry, I hope you're right but I'm not so sure. I don't know whether you know this but Sharon's been taking pills for a long time. Why, I remember seven or eight years ago, Sharon always had medication in her purse. In those days, people thought nothing of taking drugs for anxiety or insomnia. They were thought to be safe. But I've been reading recently that they're very addictive. Do you think that perhaps Sharon could be . . . ?

Harry:

Oh for goodness sake, no! She took the odd one now and then for tension but anyway they were prescribed for her. I'm sure she only took what the doctor ordered.

Louise:

Well, Harry, I don't know. Sharon and I went away for a weekend three years ago. While we were away I saw her swallowing those pills in handfuls, four at a time, at least six times a day. She'd try to hide it but it showed. Her speech was slurred and she fell asleep a lot. I was amazed that she could still function given the quantity she took. Funny, now that I think back, I remember one afternoon she was frantic to get the car. She wouldn't say why and I didn't like to ask. Afterwards, I learned she went to visit a local doctor who didn't know her. He gave her a repeat prescription and she came back with a large bottle. I know because I deliberately looked in her handbag when she was asleep. That bottle was almost empty by the time we were leaving. And, Harry, Sharon was always changing doctors. I never knew a person to go to so many. Do you suppose she could have been getting prescriptions from *all* of them?

Oh Harry! I really wish you'd get some advice. It can't be good for her to take pills like that. Maybe she's become dependent. I read that if you take them for a long time, they can make you depressed. Do you think that could be happening to Sharon?

Harry:

I'm getting advice right now. She's under medical care and he's a good doctor. I know she switched doctors a lot because she didn't always find them sympathetic. She needs someone who understands her, someone who makes it easy for her . . .

Louise:

I'm sorry to interrupt you, Harry, but I can't help wondering if Sharon told each new doctor about the others? Could she have been manipulating them to get prescriptions from a number of doctors at once? Is that possible?

Harry:

Emphatically not! Sharon likes to have a doctor she trusts. I think she's entitled to that. Anyway, Sharon's not a manipulative person. She's very gentle. She's always had a problem with tension and anxiety. I suppose she has a nervous disposition. She's always found it hard to face things. She needs protection, sheltering, someone to lean on. That's just the way she is. In fact, I like that about her. I'm glad to protect her. She needs me. I'm sure these antidepressants will work soon. Then she'll be herself again. You'll see.

Louise:

Perhaps you're right, Harry. I'm just not sure. I won't mention it again. Maybe I was intruding. If you're happy with it, I suppose it's really none of my business.

Harry:

Oh please don't feel like that, Louise. I know you and Sharon are good friends. I'm not worried about it. I don't see a problem. Let's forget it, shall we?

Correcting The Disorder Arising From Dependency

Disorder and dependency are soulmates in that crises occur frequently. They are uncontrolled and unplanned, arising as a consequence of the behavior of a problem drinker, drug-taker or gambler. Some crises involve individuals or organizations outside the family, including financial institutions and the legal system. Realistic demands are made by people to whom the troubled individual owes money or services or whom he has manipulated or disappointed by his unreliability. Affected individuals or organizations usually try to force the person with the problem to meet his obligations. They require repayment, compensation or firm commitments for the future. Such demands place the family of the dependent person under stress. Concerned persons fear the consequences of this type of involvement with legal or financial institutions. Therefore, they begin to assume responsibility for dealing with difficulties of this type. Sometimes they act as intermediaries between the dependent person and outsiders, making agreements on his behalf. They commonly assume direct responsibility for clearing the debts of the troubled individual. Their aim is to straighten things out but, in fact, this behavior protects the person with the dependency from directly facing the consequences of excessive use. Increasingly, he begins to rely on others to correct the financial, legal and work-related disorders that result from excessive use of alcohol, drugs or gambling.

Examples Of Enabling Based On Correction

Examples of enabling based on correction include the following behaviors by concerned persons:

- Taking personal responsibility for paying bills or meeting financial obligations undertaken by the troubled individual to finance his dependency.
- Arranging legal advice or using personal contacts to protect the dependent person from charges arising from behavior which breaks the law.
- Negotiating with key outsiders such as banks, doctors, employers or police on behalf of the dependent person, so that he avoids having to cope directly with realistic demands.

Correcting the disorder arising from dependency may have the following effects on the person with the problem:

- It permits the dependent person to avoid the external consequences of excessive alcohol, drug or gambling use.
- It reduces anxiety levels and creates a false sense of safety in the troubled individual.
- It contributes to increased bravado, limit-testing and an attitude of carelessness about real consequences of behavior, thereby putting the individual with the problem and the family unit increasingly at risk.

Correcting the disorder arising from dependency may have the following effects on concerned persons:

- It overburdens the family members financially if they take on debts incurred by the dependent person.
- It enmeshes concerned persons in the disorder of dependency by obliging them to manipulate outsiders.
- Anxiety arising from continuing crises creates ongoing tension in the family as long as concerned persons assume responsibility for resolving problems.
- The accumulated stress of continuing crises eventually becomes emotionally overwhelming for family members or friends. This increases the likelihood of avoidance, rather than intervention.

Enough Is Enough

Father:

I'm sick to death of you, John! You've caused more trouble than the rest of the family put together. You never could manage money. All that talk of trying to make an easy killing at the track, all those grandiose notions of big houses and yachts when you win. You can't hold on to it for long, though, can you? Straight back again — more bets, more losses. How can you be so stupid? I've been bailing you out of scrapes for the past 10 years. Do you think I'm made of money? I've paid bookies' bills, bank loans you took out, even those you took out forging my signature as guarantor. What on earth is the matter with you anyway? Why do you have to place such large bets? Why can't you just place an occasional bet like everyone else?

Well, I'm not putting up with it anymore. As far as I'm concerned, you've had your last handout. Cut out this ridiculous gambling and get a proper job like everyone else. What makes you so special? The only thing you're good at is wasting my hard-earned money. I wouldn't have paid up last time if you weren't being threatened with court proceedings. And your mother is almost out of her mind. People telephoning, looking for money you owe them. They even come to the house. She feels so ashamed. I happen to know she's used the money she was saving to visit your sister in Paris to pay your bills. I just hope you realize the sacrifice she's made. I can't afford to send her. I'm up to my eyeballs in debt paying for your foolishness.

Well, yesterday was the last straw. Some sleazy-looking character came here, making threats. Who are you associating with anyway? You don't seem to have a decent friend in the world. I want you to move, get out of our lives. Buckle down to a bit of normal living and get your head out of the clouds. Learn the value of money the hard way, the way I had to. I don't want you here any more. I've had enough! Get yourself straightened out and maybe we'll talk again, but you're on your own now. I don't care what scrapes you get yourself into. It's your problem from now on!

Compensating For The Dependent Person's Disruptive Behavior

As time passes, the dependent person becomes so preoccupied with drinking, drug-taking or gambling that he fails to fulfill important responsibilities within the family unit and at work. Absenteeism, incapacity and hangover contribute to his inability to function, leading to deterioration in these vital life areas. Sometimes the troubled individual does not participate in family life. He usually is so preoccupied with drinking, drug-taking or gambling that he pays scant attention to the emotional and practical issues which concern family members on a day-to-day basis.

Persistent inadequacy of a key person can threaten the security of the family as a unit. In the case of dependency, it is common for family members to assume more and more of the troubled individual's responsibilities. A spouse may become the family manager, operating without the continuing support of the dependent partner. Sometimes older children are involved in this process. They become adults prematurely because they share the concerns and tasks of the nondependent partner. These older children can become so preoccupied with grown-up concerns that they lose the ability to relate well to people of their own age group.

Most families reorganize to some extent in order to compensate for the troubled individual's lack of involvement. Roles change and responsibilities are reallocated, to try to ensure day-to-day stability. A similar process can occur at work. Colleagues cover up for absenteeism, correct inadequate work and minimize or divert the workload of the dependent person when he is incapable.

The process of compensation overburdens concerned persons. It also excludes the troubled individual from responsibility toward others, as he plays an increasingly less central inadequate role in the lives of those with whom he is involved. As preoccupation with chemical or gambling abuse grows, the troubled individual welcomes any reduction in his burden of responsibility within the family unit or at work. At the same time, resentment develops, due to a growing sense of exclusion and as a reaction to the angry or contemptuous attitudes of concerned persons. Self-esteem deteriorates steadily as the person with the problem experiences shame and remorse on a recurring basis. To compensate for growing feelings of inadequacy, resentful or grandiose attitudes are displayed.

The Resentful Dependent Person becomes small-minded and petty, holding grudges indefinitely and being overprotective of his dignity or rights. He makes swift and hostile judgments of others and rarely forgives and forgets. To maintain self-esteem, he has to force others to take him seriously at all times and he punishes family members, friends and acquaintances with negative attitudes and vengeful behaviors if they incur his wrath.

The Grandiose Dependent Person greatly overvalues his contribution within the family unit or at work, as well as his social position. Despite the fact that others have, of necessity, taken over essential components of his important roles, he continues to present himself in an unrealistic way. He is preoccupied with his own importance and may attach himself socially to people he desires to emulate. Unrealistic, grandiose attitudes ensure that his response to real family difficulties and growing financial problems is essentially dismissive. He always has a scheme, a plan, contacts or a pending deal. His association with people who are more financially secure, or in a higher social stratum, gives him a transient sense of belonging and acceptance. This allows him to avoid facing his growing feeling of inferiority.

Despite such unrealistic self-presentation, a dependent person who adopts either of the above postures can continue to function because people surrounding him compensate, fulfilling his essential tasks and responsibilities. In order to live with his failure to perform effectively, the troubled individual needs to denigrate the efforts of others. He becomes hostile but is completely dependent for his survival on family members and friends. Growing feelings of inadequacy lead him to resent the competence of others. He refuses to take direction or listen to guidance and will often do the opposite when a reasonable request is made of him. His fragile self-esteem gives rise to angry, contemptuous behavior to those who are close to him and hostile compliance with people who are powerful in his life.

As we can see, compensatory behaviors by family members or friends do more than simply help the dependent person avoid responsibility. They also contribute to the emergence of negative attitudes which enable the troubled individual to become emotionally isolated.

Compensating for the dependent person's disruptive behavior may include the following responses by family members and friends:

- Attempting to protect the dependent person from the emotional impact of other people's justifiable anger or disappointment with his behavior by acting as a buffer or adopting the role of peacemaker.
- Taking over the roles and functions of the dependent person so that responsibility is removed and he is eventually excluded.
- Accepting the responsibilities of dual-parent.
- Becoming a breadwinner by necessity rather than choice.
- Taking on the responsibilities of a parent while still a child in the family.
- Engaging in behavior intended to shore up the family unit, despite the constant drain on financial resources

arising from ongoing alcohol, drug or gambling abuse such as borrowing or accepting gifts of money, food, clothing or household goods from family members or friends in order to provide necessities and maintain the appearance of a normal household.

Compensating behavior by family members or friends may have the following effects on the dependent person:

- Personal responsibilities can be avoided because others cope in a difficult situation.
- It provides a cushioning effect in which reality is avoided.
- It creates a sense of exclusion and generates resentment.
- It reduces tolerance for stress, as appropriate anxiety about irresponsible behavior is dissipated by the compensating response of others.
- It labels the dependent person as inadequate, uncaring or self-absorbed.

Compensating behavior by family members or friends may have the following effects on concerned persons:

- It contributes to exhaustion, stress and a sense of aloneness.
- The reorganization of the family can create an unhealthy new balance, which does not meet the emotional and social needs of its members.

For Better Or For Worse?

I'm so tense. I'm sitting here, waiting to be interviewed. I really need this job. If I don't start earning, we've had it. Martin just doesn't bring home enough money any more. I know he's drinking — far too much. I really don't want him to feel he can't have a drink but it costs so much money. The children need new clothes and I'm always worrying about paying the grocery bills. I got such a shock recently when I read that letter from the mortgage company. Almost a year behind in our payments! They're talking of foreclosing. What would happen to us then? We'd have nowhere to go. I've got to get this job. I know I haven't worked in years. I've got nothing to offer but I'll just have to try. If I don't have an income to rely on, I'll never keep the family together. . . .

If only Martin would realize the strain it's causing. But then he's changed so much recently. He used to be really protective; wanted the best for all of us. He wanted me to stay home to look after the children. He believed that was important. So do I. I feel small children need a mother there. Maybe it's different when they go to school but I still think they need to feel someone is waiting for them. And, if I get the job, I'll have to have other people look after them when I'd prefer to do it myself. But what can I do? We need the money badly.

I can't seem to make Martin understand. Why does he need to drink so much? He's lost interest in the children lately. He used to be so good. He was a great help. He'd support me and discipline them when they needed it. Now he just falls asleep or makes completely unreasonable demands which they can't handle.

What's the matter with him? I just don't understand. He's changed so much! He was a gentle person, loving and kind. Now he's irritable with them and expects them to do things they're too young to manage. Maybe it's my fault. Perhaps I've pushed him too hard. I'm not sure. I know lately I just don't feel I have a husband any more. He's not helpful. He's out all the time and acts like a stranger when he's home. I suppose it's my responsibility to get us back on track. If I get this job, can earn my own money, I won't have to worry so much about Martin. I'll be able to take care of the family myself.

I wish I didn't have to — one of the reasons I was attracted to Martin was because he had such strong ideas about family life. Not exactly Women's Lib, I suppose, but he wanted me there. He valued and revered me in a way but things didn't work out as I planned. Maybe that's life; I don't know anymore. Right now I want more than anything to get this job. I need it! Otherwise I'm sure I'll spend months and months looking for one. If I had my own income, I'd be okay. I could take care of myself and the children. I wouldn't need Martin so much any more. I could pay the bills, provide the basics, run our household the way it ought to operate. I'd be secure then.

Martin's let us down, hasn't he? I used to think he'd be a great provider. It seems I got it wrong. Maybe my father will help? He loves the children. I'm sure he will! We'll get by — somehow.

Caretaking Of The Dependent Person

People affected by alcohol or drug dependency are sometimes physically incapable of functioning normally. Large quantities of chemicals in the body circulate to the brain and interfere with speech, vision, motor coordination and the central nervous system. When intoxicated, the dependent person may pass out, fall asleep or lose control of bodily functions. Continuing preoccupation with drinking or drug-taking may also result in neglect of personal hygiene. Such chemically-induced behavior is generally considered unacceptable among healthy adults. To preserve normal standards, concerned persons may begin caretaking — assuming responsibility for ensuring that the self-presentation of the dependent person remains within socially acceptable limits. This often becomes a serious strain as the alcohol or drug problem worsens.

Some family members risk their own safety to ensure that the person with the problem is protected from embarrassment or discomfort. Occasionally, an entire household adopts a routine geared toward normalizing the dependent person's physically uncontrolled behavior. This helps maintain a facade of normality while the family bears the brunt of the tension and distress.

The Dependent's Domination

Because of the desire to avoid conflict, concerned persons allow the disorganized behavior of the troubled individual to dominate the schedule of the household. The valid needs of other people take second place as the dependent person becomes increasingly preoccupied with maintaining his use of alcohol, drugs or gambling. Family members lose out on normal activities in two ways. They allow their schedules to be determined by the person with the problem. As a consequence, they may be slow to undertake involvements with which the troubled individual disagrees. Enjoyment within the family is also adversely affected by the dependent person's unreliability. Where plans are made, last minute changes result in disappointment for members of a family. Concerned persons can find themselves neglecting their own needs.

Enabling based on caretaking may include the following behaviors by concerned persons:

- Performing physical functions for the dependent person which he would have been able to perform if sober such as putting him to bed, cleaning him up, driving him home.
- Providing physical comforts (such as meals, clothing or a pleasant home environment) which the dependent person abuses by unappreciative behavior or to which he has contributed minimally from a financial perspective.
- Allowing the dependent person to assume a central role in the family by reorganizing daily events and activities to accommodate his demands or unreliability.

Enabling based on caretaking may have the following effects on the dependent person:

- It encourages self-centered behavior which takes little account of the needs of others.
- Being physically cared for while incapable adds to the loss of dignity involved in dependency.
- Relying on others for physical caretaking allows the dependent person to appear in control and functioning normally so that outsiders are unaware of the extent of the problem.

Enabling based on caretaking may have the following effects on concerned persons:

- It imposes continuing strain and requires a high level of vigilance. These can become detrimental to the emotional health of family members.
- It results in loss of respect for the dependent person who becomes viewed as just another child in the family.

The Minder

My mom always drank. She'd order gin by the caseful and have it delivered. Food was ordered in, too, because she didn't go out much. She was always a secret drinker. My dad was away a lot on business. He had no idea what was going on at home. Sometimes, when he came back, he'd query the liquor bills. My mom just said it was for entertainment — women friends for lunch. Dad paid — no problem. I used to wish he'd really ask, really demand an answer. He didn't seem to care enough. While he was home, my mom would cut down on her drinking and take pills instead so she could go out socially with him, for business things mostly, I think. I know she hated them but my father would have been angry if she hadn't gone.

I could never talk to my father. We weren't at all close. Oh, he was affectionate, even called me sweetheart and poppet and brought me nice presents from all the places he'd been. I badly wanted him to talk to me. He had no idea at all what it was like at home for my little brother Joey and me and he never asked. We had a cleaning lady who came three mornings a week but otherwise, nobody ever called. Mom has no relatives and Dad's live far away. It was just us — Mom, Joey and me.

Joey is younger than I am, and Mom never seemed to like him. When she'd get very drunk, she used to say he was a replica of his father. It was said spitefully and really hurt Joey. He'd cry for hours afterward. At one stage I was frantic. There had been a scene and I couldn't find him. I thought he'd run away. I was almost going to call the police when I thought of checking the attic. There he was, only six years old, curled up in an old trunk on a dusty blanket. His face was streaked with tears and he was sucking his thumb. He'd fallen asleep, exhausted. After that, I knew where to look for him when things were bad.

When my mother drank, one of two things happened. She either became incapable and passed out or she was full of furious energy. Naturally, Joey and I were her targets. She'd do a sudden inspection of our rooms and rant and rave if the smallest thing was out of place. She'd insist on supervising our homework, keeping us up really late until our vision was blurring. When she was drinking, night and day were the same to Mother. She had no concept of time or our schedules. I always got Joey ready for school in the morning because Mother was never awake. I washed and ironed our uniforms and clothes and cooked the meals.

The worst part of all was looking after Mother when she was really drunk. I was always afraid she'd fall or pass out somewhere and we wouldn't be able to get her to bed. You see, we never knew when Dad was due home and for some reason, we always felt he'd be angry with us if we hadn't looked after Mother properly. Joey worried about this a lot because Dad often said, "Take care of your mother now," when he was going away.

Sometimes Mother would drink downstairs and fall asleep on the couch. She often wet herself and I'd have to try to wash out the stain later so the cleaning lady wouldn't see. I'd try to get her into the bath and a clean nightgown. Usually by then she was sobering up. She'd shake and shiver and cry. Sometimes, she'd say she was sorry. It was horrible. I hated having to do that. It made me sick and upset for hours afterward. I always felt guilty because I couldn't love her properly.

And yet I couldn't leave her, I was always worried about her. I did really badly at school. I could never concentrate, except on the morning the cleaning lady was in. Mother made a bit of an effort then. But I always wanted to be at home in case something happened. Once she fell down the stairs. She didn't seem to be hurt but Joey and I had to try and get her to bed. It was really hard. I pulled her under the armpits and Joey tried to get her to put her legs up on each step. It took forever. Mother was cursing and Joey and I were crying.

Another night she was fumbling for a bottle in the liquor cabinet. She was unsteady on her feet and lost her balance. She grabbed the cabinet for support and pulled it down. She wasn't hurt but the mess! I still remember the smell of all those drinks mixed together as I tried to scrub the carpet. I cut my hand on a broken bottle although I really wanted to slit my mother's throat. I was exhausted. I kept waiting for the day she'd hurt herself. Part of me wished it would happen because we could call a doctor. Maybe the doctor would know what to do. I didn't.

I suppose I've made Mother sound like a dreadful person. I just never saw a good side to her at that stage. When my father was home, she'd be nice to us but it was an act. We always knew it would be the same again when he was gone. I'll never forgive my father for not noticing. As I got older, all I could think of was getting away and taking Joey with me. As far as I was concerned, we were orphans.

Supplementing The Dependent Person's Supply

When dependency is established, the person with the problem gives priority to maintaining his supply of alcohol or drugs. He is also preoccupied with ensuring that money to purchase chemicals or gamble continues to be available. To accomplish these ends the troubled individual will go to great lengths. His behavior may include cheating or stealing from others. If funds are limited, his excessive spending to maintain the dependency results in financial deprivation within the family. The person with the problem then expends a great deal of energy securing supplies. As a consequence, he may encounter serious difficulties with financial institutions or the legal system.

However, family members or friends can also become involved in procuring supplies. In some instances their participation occurs as a result of manipulation by the troubled individual. He is quick to recognize a soft touch and will placate, compliment and charm anyone in his circle who is willing to provide alcohol, drugs or funds. Sometimes concerned persons are happy to do this, rationalizing the excesses of the dependent person. Others resent it but avoid saying no because they prefer to be considered hospitable or are afraid of unpleasantness. On occasion the troubled individual will exercise a subtle tyranny, using the norms of politeness to oblige others to keep pouring or providing. Behavior of this type becomes socially unacceptable when repeated frequently. Eventually family members or friends employ avoidance tactics. They stop inviting or including the dependent person socially but rarely offer a direct explanation of their reasons. Therefore, the person with the problem is not helped to see clearly how his excessive drinking, drugtaking or gambling is alienating others.

Enabling with supplies may include the following:

- Loaning money without insisting on repayment or without confronting a person who fails to repay.
- Giving gifts of money to the dependent person which are spent on supplies.
- Providing alcohol and/or drugs for the dependent person's use.
- Purchasing alcohol and drugs or placing bets on behalf of the dependent person.
- Permitting thefts of household goods or money to go unchallenged, when the dependent person is known to be responsible.

That's What Friends Are For

Well, Sam was my friend, wasn't he? Naturally, I'd help him out if I could. Sometimes, he'd get a little stuck financially. I'd always help him out. I wouldn't feel good refusing him. Usually, he didn't pay me back but then he had all those expenses, the kids at school and the mortgage. I'm single so I don't have to worry about things like that. Actually, I used to feel kind of sorry for him. He had all these problems and, between ourselves, I don't think things were going too well at home. His wife seemed pretty demanding, always wanting the best, the latest appliances, a bigger house. He was under an awful lot of pressure.

The only time he could let his hair down was when a couple of the guys got together. Sam would come over to my place and we'd really tie one on. Sam drank a lot more than the rest of us. He liked whiskey while we all drank beer. But I always made sure I had enough for him. I felt I was helping him relax.

Odd thing, though, he didn't always relax. Sometimes, he'd get a bit hard to handle — a kind of personality change, I suppose. He used to beef a lot about his wife. To be honest, we all got kind of tired listening but he seemed to be letting off steam and we thought it would do him good.

He could drink though. I never saw anybody handle so much alcohol. But then, of course, he's a pretty big fellow. Must have a hollow leg. He rarely had a hangover in the morning either, not like the rest of us. Even so, if there was still booze in the morning before he left, he'd finish it — first thing. Well, just so long as he enjoyed himself.

Funny, though, Sam and I have been close for a long time but he's never invited me to his house. I haven't even seen a photograph of his wife. I imagine her as some kind of battle-ax. I wonder what she's really like? Hell, maybe I'm better off. The way Sam talks about her, she sounds like bad news.

Enabling: Conclusion

Some enabling behaviors are necessary for the survival of the family unit, particularly to provide for the well-being and security of children. Most families enable to some extent. The type of enabling which gets greatest emphasis varies considerably from situation to situation. It depends, to some extent, on the pattern of use of the troubled individual. Where alcohol, drug or gambling abuse occur primarily outside the family, control-based enabling may be limited to contesting behaviors on the part of concerned persons. Protection of the dependency is common. Concealing and rationalizing usually occur, while caretaking may or may not be a feature of the family response. Correcting tends to occur at some stage, though repetition of the disordered behavior can result in early abandonment of this course of action. Compensating behavior usually occurs in some form.

Stopping Support

To ensure successful recovery, it is essential that concerned persons take steps to stop their inadvertent support of the active dependency. Until the cat and mouse control game (with its constant arguments and tensions) ends or the props provided by concerned persons' protection are no longer available, the troubled individual is not forced to recognize that he has lost control. Many people in difficulty with alcohol, drugs or gambling have sought help following crises. Some are motivated solely by self-protection. Others genuinely experience a moment of truth when faced with unpleasant consequences. The remainder, hopefully, are encouraged to seek help by nonenabling family members or friends who care enough to work toward intervention.

Sometimes the troubled individual secretly welcomes the intervention of others, having been unable to stop alone and feeling incapable of asking for help. As dependency progresses, the defense system becomes increasingly rigid and all-pervasive. It creates a barrier to the reception of reality-based information about the impact on others and the personal consequences of continuing alcohol, drug or gambling abuse. Before defenses exclude reality completely, there is sometimes a period of awareness during which the dependent person can acknowledge excessive use to himself, though rarely to others. He feels unease and a growing anxiety about his loss of control. However, at this time, chemical abuse is still largely rewarding and the familial and societal conse-

quences of continuing abuse not yet fully experienced. As the
dependent person sees it, there is no real reason to stop. At
this stage, too, abstinence would be perceived as deprivation,
that is, the loss of a rewarding experience.

The Defense System

As abuse continues and compulsion becomes overwhelming, disordered behavior and unpleasant personality changes
are increasingly in evidence. Now the defense system becomes essential, both to protect the dependency from the
threat other people pose and to protect the self-esteem of
the troubled individual. In order to live with himself, he
must stifle his awareness of the implications of dependency-
induced behavior. Feelings of shame, remorse, guilt and
self-hatred are excluded from conscious awareness. Emotional responsiveness diminishes. Chemicals have replaced
people as a source of gratification and he needs to repeat
the experience constantly to get the effect he requires.

The firmly entrenched defense system limits the self-awareness of the dependent person, making it increasingly difficult
to relate effectively to others or to accomplish tasks in a realistic way. Difficult or anxiety-provoking demands are avoided,
while rationalizations are employed to avoid guilt or shame.
Day-to-day behavior becomes totally drug or gambling-cen-
tered, as the compulsion becomes increasingly dominant.
Family life, relationships, productivity at work are progressively affected in a deteriorating way. Episodes of panic and
fear occur regularly as the defense system temporarily breaks
down, flooding the troubled individual with normally buried
emotions. During such moments of self-knowledge, some
dependent people are aware of loss of control and of the
destructive effects of chemicals or gambling. Avowals to cut
back, limit intake or regain control are made privately and
are often followed by serious attempts to implement changes
in pattern and frequency of abuse. Sincere attempts of this
kind are ineffective, however, because the illness has now
progressed to a point where a commitment to abstinence is
essential if freedom from compulsion is to occur.

Abuse continues and the defense system remains intact in terms of the troubled individual's observable response to others. However, behavioral disorder and deteriorating relationships now feature prominently in the dependent person's life. Each drinking, drug-taking or gambling day brings its own failure, manipulation, mental confusion and frightening consequences. While defenses are still used automatically under threat and continue to contribute to self-delusion, they no longer work effectively to protect the person with the problem from awareness of emotional pain. He feels bad all the time and drinking, drug-taking or gambling no longer provide the high he continues to seek. He is in despair, depressed and desperate, though these feelings, too, are concealed from others.

He tries to regain control by stopping for a while but without appropriate help, most dependent people feel even worse without chemicals at this stage of the illness. Once again, the troubled individual is aware of his need for help, though he may not associate his pervasive emotional distress with chemical abuse. He still remembers the "days of wine and roses," when alcohol, drugs or gambling were consistently rewarding. He believes their use holds the key to his state of mind. If he could just find the formula, he'd feel good again.

Despite the rigidity of defenses, his desperation leaks occasionally. He will complain to others of feeling depressed, futile, overburdened, though he usually feels this to be related to unhappiness in relationships or dissatisfaction with the direction of his life, rather than alcohol, drug or gambling abuse. He knows he needs help but he doesn't know the type of help he needs. His family, his friends, his colleagues at work can help him best by intervention. They can see the problem; he cannot. But his inner misery requires some balm. Abstinence and recovery can provide that. His defenses, despair and lack of awareness of the connection between chemical abuse and emotional pain make intervention a necessity at this stage.

We will discuss defensiveness later in more detail but right now, we are ready to move on to look at nonenabling and intervention, so that we can begin to understand what is involved in adopting this course of action.

Insight — Enabling Awareness

Carol (to alcoholism counselor):

I'm amazed. I can't believe I've learned so much just by talking to you. You know, I really didn't want to come today. I resented it. I felt, "Why should I? Joe has the problem, not me; I'm not drinking too much." Then I thought, "Well, at least someone will listen to me; let me talk about Joe." I get so few chances to let off steam.

You know, it's funny. I wanted to talk about Joe but we ended up talking about me. In a way, I'm glad. I know my doctor's been worried about me. That's why he suggested I come here. I suppose I have been pretty tense lately. I'm tired all the time and I don't like the way I behave toward the children. I'm so snappy and irritable. Only the other day I realized my four-year-old son is frightened of me — I was shouting at him for nothing — almost screaming. I felt so ashamed. That's not like me . . . I've changed so much.

These last few years have been a nightmare, constantly worrying about Joe, our future and the children. I felt trapped and I really couldn't see a way out. You've been so helpful to me. I see things in a completely different light now. I realize I can do something constructive — something that will really help. Do you know, I never even knew about intervention? Isn't that amazing? When I think about it, I didn't even realize Joe could be an alcoholic and could get help. I've been living with the problem for so long but I just didn't *see* it properly.

While we were talking, I began to realize that I've been mishandling the whole thing. I didn't mean to . . . I never knew about enabling until today. But I see now, that's just what I was doing. For years I've protected Joe, lied for him, borrowed money from my father to take care of his bills, made excuses to everyone for his drinking . . . I covered up for him because I was so afraid he'd lose his job. I used to hate telephoning on Monday morning to say he wasn't coming in. It was so hard to keep on lying. I can hardly believe I did all that and for so long.

I felt I had to keep Joe's drinking a secret, from our friends and my own family. I used to have friends of my own but I just dropped out of things. I couldn't face people and I didn't want to have to talk about Joe. You know how people ask . . . It's just politeness but they assume you're a couple and do things together. These last few years, I felt I couldn't rely on Joe for anything. We never go out together anymore because I just can't stand his drinking. I've been feeling so isolated, so cut off from people. It's as though Joe's drinking is the center of my world. A day is good or bad, depending on Joe and his drinking.

I suppose now that I understand enabling, I realize how hard I've been trying to stop Joe's drinking. Every day is a battle. I nag, I plead, I issue ultimatums. He promises and I believe him. Then when he drinks again, I feel devastated.

"He can't possibly love me," I think. "How could he keep doing this to me if he did?" And then I feel such a failure, a bad wife, unlovable. I blame myself but I'm so angry with Joe as well.

You know, when you talked about compulsion and about alcoholism as an illness, it really changed the way I see things. I thought Joe could control himself, if he wanted to or if I forced him. Now I see he can't, that he's out of control and he needs help. I've been doing all the wrong things.

When you showed me that list of enabling behaviors, I recognized so many — I've been doing them for years. I'd try one thing to control him — then I'd try another and I always protected him. I understand now why they didn't work but at the time, I'd feel so angry and frustrated.

I hated Joe. I couldn't talk to him. Lately I feel he's almost another child in the family because I have to take so much responsibility. I've been feeling such contempt for him. I just didn't realize he was ill and needed help. I thought I was helping him but now I see my type of help is not what he needs. In spite of everything, I still love Joe. We were really happy when we first married and he was a wonderful person. We seemed to have such a great future . . . . He's changed, too. Sometimes I feel I'm living with a stranger.

He says such hurtful things when he's drunk. You know, before coming here, I was beginning to think we had a marital problem, that perhaps we should separate, that we weren't right for each other. Now I see it differently. Joe is an alcoholic and he needs help to stop drinking and to get his thinking and feelings back to normal.

I need help, too. Now that I understand, I plan to stop enabling. I realize now I was just creating tension for myself and the children and I was also alienating Joe. I'd like to help him but I'm not sure how easy it will be. I'll need support but, really, after all these years it will be such a relief to feel I'm doing something constructive. Intervention is really the only option we have.

4

Enabling Reversal —
From Enabler To Intervener

Some people hesitate to stop enabling because of misconceptions about the changes entailed. For example, becoming nonenabling does not mean excluding the dependent person from family life. Nor is it necessary to develop an atmosphere of criticism in which the problem behavior is constantly scrutinized. A nonenabling family does not abandon the troubled person. Rather, it strips him of the crutches and rationalizations which contribute to self-delusion. When enabling ends, the dependent person is forced to "own" his behavior and its distressing consequences. He becomes open to the recognition that the problem is personal and requires self-help. When control and protection by others no longer occur, the troubled individual is increasingly aware of compulsion, powerlessness and despair. Sooner or later, perhaps following a crisis, an offer of help is accepted — because no alternative remains.

What Is A Nonenabling Environment?

Ideally, relatives and friends deliberately choose not to engage in control-based enabling. In effect, they stop trying to prevent further abuse of alcohol, drugs or gambling, no longer protecting the dependent person from the consequences of behavior occurring because of excessive use.

At its most basic, ending enabling involves stopping both the control game and the protection of the troubled individual.

While these initial steps are valuable, their impact on the dependent person is lessened unless the enabling process is completely reversed. This requires the adoption of intervention-orientated behavior by family members and friends.

Enabling reversal assumes an active, informed approach by concerned persons. A basic prerequisite of enabling reversal is acceptance of the illness of addiction and a belief that outside help is required. It is essential to care enough for the troubled individual to try to "reach" him. Most families use a combination of support, feedback, influence and sometimes leverage.

The creation of a recovery-oriented family atmosphere in which it is uncomfortable for the troubled individual to continue destructive behavior is the first step. Ideally, this is coupled with a workable plan using an appropriate source of help when the dependent person is ready. These strategies work best where there is less emphasis on persuading the troubled person to stop drinking, drug-taking or gambling and more on inducing him to agree to start a recovery process.*

Sometimes concern alone is not sufficient to break through the dependent person's compulsion and defensiveness. In fact, used alone, expressions of concern can be misinterpreted by the person with the problem. Caring statements by others allow him to feel accepted and encourage him to defer a serious assessment of his difficulties. Concern is the motivating factor in an intervention attempt

---

Based on the ideas of Roque Fajardo in *Helping Your Alcoholic Before He Or She Hits Bottom* (New York: Crown Publishers, 1976).

which, when used in combination with other strategies, leads to success. Offering feedback to the dependent person, setting limits and using crises constructively underline the losses and damage involved in continuing to abuse alcohol, drugs or the gambling experience.

Ideally, concerned persons learn to become nonenabling in a sincere effort to make it necessary for the troubled individual to seek and use help. Ending enabling, then, is an important part of a behavioral plan to achieve intervention and assist in the recovery of the dependent person.

Freedom from enabling also has a personal function for family members and friends. Becoming nonenabling restores time and energy to people who have neglected normal needs in their efforts to tackle the problems posed by dependency. Even the strongest concerned persons become fatigued and self-depreciating following repeated, unsuccessful attempts to control and protect the individual in difficulty. Therefore, before long, there are several emotionally-distressed people in a family, rather than just one. When enabling ends there is time for constructive self-care and mutual support, since the focus of daily activity no longer centers on the dependent person and his problem. Asserting personal rights and meeting needs, where possible, help sustain concerned persons while they concentrate on intervention and recovery.

What Is Intervention?

We shall take a closer look at some of the changes necessary to reverse enabling later. At this point it seems appropriate to ask: *What is intervention? Basically it includes any deliberate, constructive effort by family members, friends or colleagues to persuade the troubled person to seek outside advice and help with his problem.*

Actively dependent people usually need professional guidance and often require residential treatment. Some do very well in self-help groups, such as Alcoholics Anonymous, Narcotics Anonymous and Gamblers Anonymous, particularly if they have had medical care prior to stopping. However, the first step in beginning a recovery process involves an evaluation of the extent of the difficulty by a person or group with expertise in the area. Professionals, or people who themselves share the problem but have recovered, have the authority of knowledge. They therefore can go further than concerned persons in helping the troubled individual accept that he is dependent and cannot recover alone. It is important for relatives and friends to recognize that the full burden of handling the problem responsibly does not fall on them. They have a vital role, in that they are most directly involved with the dependent person and most personally affected by his behavior. As such, family members and friends make a unique contribution to recovery.

However, dependency requires support from outside the family. Self-help groups for dependent people and their equivalents for concerned persons (i.e. Al-Anon, Gamanon, Nar-Anon) are essential sources of input when coping with an alcohol, drug or gambling problem.

Many recovering people need an initial period of professional treatment before they can successfully utilize self-help programs. Many families need guidance to decide whether a period of treatment is appropriate. Participation in a good program, specifically designed to meet the needs of both dependent and concerned persons, can give the newly-recovering individual and his family a head start. This increases the chance of "contented sobriety" and, of course, benefits everyone in the long term.

Despite the potential benefits, choosing intervention as an option is not always easy for concerned persons. There are issues to be considered and, possibly, resistance to be overcome before it becomes possible to wholeheartedly pursue this course of action. Here it might be helpful to examine some typical assumptions families make about dependency. These can be discarded on examination because they are based on false premises.

He's Just Doing It To Hurt Me
Or Because He Doesn't Care

The first assumption to challenge is that the dependent person is being willfully self-destructive and is deliberately choosing to behave in a selfish, embarrassing or uncaring way. He may sometimes indeed behave badly as an angry response to other people's efforts to keep him under control. More usually, however, the dependent person's behavior is linked with certain symptoms of the illness.

Compulsion

Compulsion is a central element in the illness. It is the feature which makes willpower irrelevant while the dependency is active. Willpower permits choice; compulsion implies need. As the illness progresses, a dependent person becomes incapable of using alcohol, drugs or gambling in a reasonable, nondamaging way. Compulsion is usually experienced as an overwhelming desire to drink, take drugs or gamble, which takes no account of appropriateness or reality. The thought creates the impetus to act, despite the unpleasant consequences of the action. Willpower, logic and self-interest become secondary to this powerful drive to continue use — even at the risk of behaving irresponsibly. Compulsion, then, is often experienced as an irrational craving which determines behavior and which is too forceful to resist on an ongoing basis.

Increased Intake

Compulsion is linked with another important element in dependency — the inability to maintain control of alcohol, drug or gambling use. When chemicals are abused regularly, the body becomes habituated to the quantity consumed. Therefore, the desired mood change requires an increased intake as time goes by. A phase of high tolerance usually ensues. The dependent person consumes large quantities without appearing to be affected physiologically, for instance, in terms of speech, motor coordination and vision. At some point the person with the problem becomes unable to stop, until unconsciousness or lack of funds terminate an episode. At this point the dependency becomes highly conspicuous. When diagnosing dependency, current and previous tolerance levels are evaluated. In addition, evidence of loss of control and compulsion are sought as important indices to the presence of the illness.

Compulsion and loss of control are the elements in active dependency which make control-based enabling unproductive. "Cutting back," "using will-power," "drinking socially" become increasingly difficult as the condition progresses. Despite this, some dependent people are capable of stopping temporarily when under pressure or in an attempt to disprove loss of control either to themselves or others. Such dry periods are usually accompained by a sense of deprivation with accompanying irritability and tension. The troubled individual remains preoccupied with chemicals, even though he is, technically, alcohol- or drug-free. Soon he will begin to abuse again. Retaining long-term control of consumption patterns or gambling is impossible in active dependency. When concerned persons accept this, they can shift perspective and concentrate on helping the troubled individual accept the need for outside help.

Disinhibition

The physical effect of heavy alcohol or drug intake or the mood change induced by gambling increases the likelihood of impulsive or aggressive behavior by the dependent person. In a sober state, we can exercise control over our impulses and actions. We automatically anticipate consequences and make realistic choices about our behavior. Many choices are made within a social context, as we consider how others will respond to our decisions. We also have an internal self-monitor linked with our system of values. This encourages us to choose behavior which is unlikely to create guilt or embarrassment and with which we feel personally comfortable. Under the influence of chemically-induced mood changes the dependent person's ability to control hostile or self-gratifying impulses is greatly reduced. There is an increased likelihood of verbal aggression including sarcasm, indiscreet disclosures or home truths delivered to others in an irresponsible, hurtful way. Physical aggression may occur and will often be directed at those closest to the dependent person. Sexual disinhibition is common, increasing the likelihood of inappropriate verbal or behavioral expression of sexual impulses. Judgment also is impaired, resulting in reckless or impulsive behavior and a lack of concern for normal standards of safety and the protection of self and others.

A disinhibited dependent person may behave in a way which is uncharacteristic, frightening and offensive to others. Family members and friends begin to think in terms of *Jekyll and Hyde* personality changes. They increasingly see the troubled individual as a hostile, terrifying stranger when "under the influence." Tragically, the dependent person is seldom fully aware of the extent to which his behavior deteriorates in such circumstances. There are a number of elements within dependency which distort his view of self and reality.

Distorted Thinking And Defensiveness

Distorted, unrealistic and sometimes illogical thinking patterns manifest themselves with increasing frequency as a dependency progresses. To an informed observer, the troubled person appears to reconstruct reality in order to explain inappropriate patterns of behavior and his growing obsession with alcohol, drug or gambling use. Family members or friends, however, may be affected more personally. They begin to doubt their own judgments and perceptions of events and become drawn in to accepting the troubled individual's interpretation. Eventually they, too, can become unrealistic about personal needs, self-concept and the welfare of the family unit.

Several elements contribute to distorted thinking during an active dependency. Amnesic episodes are common even among compulsive gamblers. The effect of chemicals on the brain interferes with memory. Episodes of drinking, drug-taking or gambling are forgotten, despite the fact that the dependent person behaved in an alert, apparently normal way. These gaps in memory create distortion since the troubled individual is unaware of behavior occurring during blank periods. Large quantities of alcohol or drugs in the system also interfere with concentration and accurate attention to the immediate environment. This results in confusion and forgetfulness.

Euphoria

The mood-change associated with alcohol, drug or gambling use is, initially, positive and pleasurable — a high. The sense of euphoria is valued and sought with increasing frequency. The connection between drinking/drug-taking/ gambling and this pleasurable subjective feeling state is reinforced by constant repetition. Eventually it is learned so well that it becomes an unshakable belief — *Alcohol makes me feel good*. For this reason, euphoria is remembered as the dominant feature, despite the unacceptable or manipulative behavior associated with episodes of use. This type of distortion is built in to dependency.

When dependency is well advanced, euphoria is replaced by distress or oblivion as the positive, chemically-induced mood change becomes increasingly elusive. Despite experiencing pain instead of pleasure as a result of drinking or drug-taking, the dependent person continues to anticipate the return of the high. He will often experiment with more powerful drugs or combinations of alcohol and drugs in an attempt to re-experience euphoria. "Euphoric recall" then encourages the dependent person to disregard his currently unpleasant experience of alcohol, drug use or gambling. It also makes him unaware of the need to take constructive steps to deal with the problem.

The growing dependency also stimulates the development of defensiveness in the person with the problem. The protection of alcohol, drug or gambling use becomes increasingly important as compulsion develops. Family members, friends, employers and authority figures are perceived as threatening since they disapprove of or are affected by excessive use. They may also be in a position to implement sanctions for unacceptable behavior. The troubled individual uses defensiveness automatically and may have little or no awareness of his increasingly distorted thinking processes. Minimizing, denying, blaming and rationalizing are used routinely to placate others or divert attention from the increasing prioritization of alcohol, drug use or gambling.

Defenses are unconsciously used to protect the dependent person's self-esteem. Painful memories of inappropriate behavior induced by excessive use create guilt and remorse. The associated disapproval of others generates anxiety, fear and self-loathing. Such feelings are too painful to endure on a regular basis so the mind works automatically to protect itself from unbearable pain. When we bury feelings we can't face, we avoid reality. We also become detached because we simply don't allow ourselves to feel deeply any more. The dependent person eventually becomes quite shut off from others, locked in a world in which the protection of the chemical remains central. Emotional isolation results, with family members and friends feeling increasingly excluded.

Defensiveness makes the dependent person unapproachable and unreasonable. Eventually those who surround the troubled individual find their feelings of love and attachment evaporating in the face of his persistently unpleasant, self-engrossed behavior. By now the dependent person can no longer share with others a normal approach to living and emotional involvement. His ability to respond in an appropriate way has been eroded by the emotional changes and defensiveness typical of active dependency. He also believes his own defenses and is unable to see the realistic basis for concerned persons' anxiety about his well-being and behavior.

Behind the wall of defenses surrounding the troubled individual, most actively dependent people feel increasingly worthless as the illness progresses. They are remorseful about behavior which conflicts with their sober or normal expectations of themselves. They can also feel ashamed of their failure to become the type of partner, parent, friend or employee they may once have wanted to be. Eventually remorse and self-hatred are routinely experienced and often spill over in personal attacks on vulnerable people in the user's family, social or work environment. Relatives and friends, at the receiving end of unwarranted hostility, find it hard not to view this behavior as indicative of madness or badness. Difficult as it is to understand, distorted feelings of this type become quite commonplace as the illness progresses. The "crazy stranger," who says or does hurtful things, has become emotionally sick as a result of dependency. Inside the person you may once have known and loved remains a prisoner of his compulsion to protect the alcohol, drug-use or gambling at all costs.

The symptoms outlined above accompany most active dependencies. Therefore, it is particularly important for concerned persons to understand and accept the illness. When you believe that the troubled individual is out of control and needs help, you may find your concern re-emerging to replace the distance and anger of recent years. This does not imply that your anger has no place in the recovery process. You have a right to your feelings and often anger is the appropriate emotion when somebody is being consistently disruptive. You should not, however, allow continuing anger to blind you to the facts of the illness or to permit you to feel justified in not responding to the dependent person's need for help.

The Role Of Family And Friends

Family members and friends are central figures in the intervention, treatment and recovery process and an attitude of concern is basic to success. Sometimes, following years of futile effort to correct the problem, concerned persons begin to view the situation as hopeless. Working toward recovery usually is not easy. There are mixed emotions: hope, often dampened by the recollection of past failures; a fervent wish to succeed, countered by an understandable reluctance to risk disappointment yet again; lack of trust in the apparently uncaring dependent person, counterbalanced by a longing for the "person we once knew." We must recognize that we often feel ambivalent undertaking a course of action with an uncertain outcome, especially one which requires a lot of effort. It also is quite usual to feel reluctant to love and trust again, particularly in light of past abuses. However, concerned persons may be helped to commit themselves to a recovery process by recognizing that it may bring personal benefit.

Recovery creates the possibility of a new life for everyone directly involved with the dependency. Not surprisingly, many people who have been helped to recover feel grateful to those who stood by them. With the clear thinking made possible by the alcohol-, drug- or gambling-free lifestyle, people in recovery can later come to see the valuable gift offered by concerned persons — their courage and commitment in following through with intervention in spite of hostility and denial. Love and support, unappreciated at the time, often are interpreted as pressure or interference. Yet they are helpful in rebuilding the dependent person's self-esteem and lifting the mantle of isolation with which troubled people surround themselves. Families which work together to achieve lasting recovery often renew damaged bonds. They feel increasing closeness and satisfaction with relationships when recovery becomes established. The experience of coping successfully with the problem can create a deep appreciation of the normality of the new life. It also engenders a sense of confidence in dealing with any future difficulties or life crises.

It's My Responsibility

I feel responsible for the problem. I've added to it in some way and now I have to live with it.

Given our present state of knowledge, we no longer believe that there is one single cause of an established alcohol, drug or gambling problem. Current thinking suggests that a problem of this type emerges as a result of a combination of factors. Personality traits, bodily response to alcohol or drugs and social support of heavy drinking, drug-taking or gambling all contribute. So, too, do stressful events and conflicts within the individual's life.

We often meet sad and anxious dependent people whose self-esteem is low or who have experienced serious difficulty coping with living. The use of alcohol, drugs or gambling can initially bring relief and a sense of ease. Chemicals quickly become an important prop in the daily struggle to survive. Other nondependent people with similar difficulties resolve problems constructively by developing personal resources. Sometimes people become dependent largely because a work or social environment encourages regular use. There may be little evidence of prior personality or emotional difficulties or problems in relationships.

The issue is complex, rather than simple, yet many family members, friends and dependent people, too, spend hours agonizing about causes. The assumption is: "If we can only work out what is wrong, things will be back to normal again." This is not necessarily so, particularly where the classic symptoms of dependency are present. When these exist and can be diagnosed, the illness has become an entity in itself. It then has to be treated in its own right. No individual is directly responsible for its creation, not even the troubled person.

It therefore is necessary to avoid adopting the belief that you have, single-handedly, created the problem. Nobody could live with an actively dependent person without saying or doing something to make matters worse. To be reasonable we must acknowledge that few people know how to handle the situation constructively and most wear themselves out feeling guilty and responsible because nothing improves.

There comes a point when it is counterproductive to continue to feel blame because it affects a concerned person's energy level and self-esteem. If you are to intervene successfully, you need to feel purposeful and good about yourself. You also need the strength to cope.

Nothing Else I Can Do

I feel worthless and overwhelmed. None of my efforts to improve things has worked. There is nothing further I can do.

As a family member or friend of a dependent person, you have a central role in his life. You are hurt and damaged largely because there is an intense bond between you and the troubled individual. He feels most guilty about failing you because you have priority in his emotions. He will attack vigorously and withhold himself most from the very people with whom he has the deepest association. This is simply because you represent the greatest threat to his dependency.

In most societies there are guidelines for appropriate behavior. Even in periods of rapid social change we continue to have expectations of those who occupy certain social and familial roles. As a family member or friend, you understandably feel bad because the dependent individual fails to meet behavioral standards. However, you can safely assume that he, too, is remorseful at some level. Without consciously acknowledging his motives, a troubled person protects himself from guilt and unease by undermining and attacking others who require him to function normally. Usually he feels incapable of meeting their standards due to his preoccupation with alcohol, drugs or gambling.

Even unpleasant or dismissive behavior tells you that you are important in the dependent person's life. If you hope for recovery, you have to learn to use your position in the relationship. Family members and friends who feel particularly worthless and beaten sometimes find, on reflection, that they have been engaging in a contest of wills arising from their attempt to control the problem. Others are subject to aggression and unrelenting personal attack, which diminish their belief in themselves. In both instances, concerned persons are giving the troubled individual the power to control their inner feelings by his behavior.

We all need people in our lives who affirm us and help us feel good about ourselves. In a close relationship it is reasonable to expect that partner, parent or friend will fulfill this role. Due to the emotional changes characteristic of the illness, some dependent people are temporarily unable to feel and express care for others. In these circumstances, vulnerable concerned persons may allow themselves to feel unlovable.

Even though the behavior and demands of the troubled individual are sometimes quite unreasonable and would be difficult to tolerate under any circumstances, family members and friends will sometimes exhaust themselves trying to respond to impossible requests or conflicting messages. When they fail, they question their own competence. It would be more useful to recognize the *no-win* situation.

Restoring Self-Worth

The first step in restoring self-worth is to stop giving the dependent person the power to make you doubt yourself in a serious way. You do need others to confirm that you are worthwhile but while you are waiting for recovery, you can maintain yourself by seeking support in other relationships, such as those available in Al-Anon, Nar-Anon and Gamanon.

While confirmation of our personal worth by others is important, it is not the only source of positive self-esteem. We have a right to feel good about ourselves when we live by reasonable standards. We damage our sense of self-worth when we feel we have behaved in a manner which is personally unacceptable to us. This is a frequent source of diminished self-esteem among concerned persons.

Sometimes in the cut and thrust of active dependency you behave in a way which is out of character. You may find you're beginning to dislike yourself. Perhaps you've become irritable, nagging, withdrawn, self-pitying, morose, impetuous, aggressive or domineering. You feel guilty because you no longer approve of your behavior.

You can, however, choose how you present yourself to others. You can stop self-defeating or negative behavior simply by deciding that it's not worth the price tag — remorse or personal unease. Furthermore, by selecting courses of action that make you feel good and contribute to other peoples' comfort, you can revitalize your self-esteem and become self-confirming. When you've handled things well and are satisfied with yourself, you feel good, whatever the circumstances. This source of positive self-esteem continues to be available to you no matter how the dependent person behaves.

I Don't Want To Be Disloyal

It's disloyal of me to talk about him behind his back.

Loyalty is undoubtedly a very important quality in a relationship and sometimes we choose to sacrifice our need to confide in others to avoid breaking faith with a partner, parent or friend. Usually, however, when people have a shared secret, they talk together and support each other emotionally. In this way, neither is left without an outlet for anxieties associated with the problem.

As we know, the illness of dependency involves denial and extreme self-protectiveness on the part of the troubled person. He fails to see the problem due to his defensiveness and is usually unwilling to discuss his difficulties with others. Even when discussion occurs, the scope of conversation is limited. The dependent person's goal is to allay the fears of family members and friends about his excessive drinking, drug-taking or gambling. Exchanges of this type are rarely supportive or anxiety-reducing for concerned persons. Promises to control the problem can bring temporary reassurance but distress mounts again when there is no follow through. There is little comfort in discussing the alcohol, drug or gambling problem with the troubled individual in the hope of achieving the closeness necessary to compensate for the absence of alternative supports.

A loyal concerned person who hides the problem often becomes isolated, depressed or physically ill due to suppressed emotion. An active dependency creates crisis after crisis. There is uncertainty, fear, self-doubt and confusion for family members and friends. They need intensive support and sound guidance if they are to cope and avoid becoming emotional casualties.

Bringing the problem into the open in a constructive way is often an enormous relief. Talking things through with supportive people brings immediate reassurance. It may also help clarify the problem. Sometimes family members and friends need the encouragement of others before they can bring themselves to approach a source of help, such as a professional person, a treatment center or Al-Anon, Gam-anon or Nar-Anon. To seek guidance in this way does not indicate disloyalty. In the first place, concerned persons have the right to protect their emotional health by obtaining support. Second, professionals or self-help groups under-stand the nature of the problem and are committed to help-ing, rather than making judgments.

Avoiding discussion of the dependency out of loyalty may also prolong the problem. As the condition progresses, the troubled individual experiences increasing difficulty main-taining a facade of normal functioning. He will usually begin to deteriorate in terms of bodily health, personality, social position and employability. Once concerned persons open up and seek information, they learn that dependency is a treatable illness. As new facts are assimilated by family members and friends, it becomes clear that loyalty and commitment are best expressed through intervention. This way, the dependent person is given an opportunity to re-cover and live a fulfilling life.

In terms of constructive self-care, opening oneself to in-put and guidance from others by talking, rather than hiding, begins the healing process for concerned persons. It also gives people access to an important support network.

Ambivalence

I'd have to feel certain it was right before I could go ahead with intervention.

Ambivalence is one of the most common emotional states concerned persons experience when considering their op-tions during active dependency. There are conflicting feel-ings about the troubled person and misgivings about making the effort to intervene. An internal voice repeats, "Why should I?" while another whispers, "I ought to." You may feel wary at the very idea of implementing a plan. Perhaps you even temporarily hate the person who suggests it. Sometimes you wish you'd never learned about dependency as an illness because then you could feel angry and mistreated without conflict. Still, hope flickers. Part of you wants to go ahead while the other part resents the necessity for further change. Initially, intervention appears to involve new learning, serious rethinking and, perhaps, emotional upheaval. At some point over the years, you've become self-protective. Once you felt raw and aching; recently you've been calmer, less affected, more detached. Why start again? Why put in energy and effort which may come to nothing? Why risk further disappointment?

These are very real questions for family members and friends affected by an active dependency. Ambivalence is natural in any situation where change involves effort and the outcome is unknown. We all find it hard to tolerate conflict, yet often our emotions fluctuate. In our world we are taught to make up our minds and indecisiveness is considered a fault to be eliminated. Yet "black or white," "stop or go" attitudes equip us poorly to survive in real life. The ability to tolerate uncertainty and to acknowledge conflicting impulses are essential while working to resolve important issues. It is not wrong to have mixed feelings, as long as you accept them and don't make a premature decision to avoid inner turmoil. The process of working things through clarifies alternatives and eventually permits choice. Acknowledging and resolving ambivalence about intervention is part of the decision-making process when concerned persons are uncertain of their commitment to a new approach.

In making a choice, familiarization and necessity help family members and friends. As you think over new ideas and courses of action, your mind becomes acclimatized. Soon they begin to seem reasonable rather than threatening. You may continue to feel anxiety about change but it doesn't immobilize you any longer. Optimism has now entered the picture as a counterbalance. Now you feel: "Perhaps it could work," "Imagine if it did," "It's worth a chance, isn't it?" At this stage, you are beginning to see advantages to the new course of action. You may gradually find that the potential benefits of change outweigh the disadvantages. In choosing intervention, family members and friends are encouraged by the knowledge that it is a constructive and responsible approach to the problem.

Sometimes we make final choices out of necessity. If there is no real reason to resolve an issue, then we can consider alternatives indefinitely. In the case of dependency, the condition progresses, circumstances worsen and a point is reached where something has to be done. Then an intervention plan may be chosen because, on balance, change is seen as more desirable than the *status quo*.

When To Intervene

Some concerned persons have no difficulty whatsoever deciding to intervene. In fact, they can be glad to learn that there are guidelines available with the prospect of eventual recovery as a reward. For those who have problems making the choice, the associated confusion and uncertainty can cause stress and interfere with constructive self-care. Commitment to a plan is essential for successful intervention. Decision-making is made easier by straightforward acknowledgment of conflict. If you remain sufficiently open-minded to give full consideration to each option, eventually you will find yourself drawn to one alternative rather than another.

As you may know, current thinking about alcohol, drug and gambling dependency suggests that intervention should occur as early as possible to minimize damage to all concerned. However, when relatives and friends continue to have difficulty committing themselves to the idea of intervention, they may be better to wait rather than make a half-hearted attempt. Concerned persons who are certain that the troubled individual needs help and who have firmly decided to pursue that goal are often successful. This is not simply because of the strategies they learn to use but because of their changed view of the family situation. It's no longer *his* problem only. It's become *our* problem and people work together to encourage the troubled individual to approach a source of help.

If, however, you finally decide against intervention at the present time, do consider the idea again at a future date. Your feelings and circumstances may change. If *now or never* doesn't seem right for you, then at least let it be *if not now, sometime*.

Meanwhile, you can start taking care of yourself constructively, so that you experience a renewal of energy and improved self-esteem. You will find some suggestions in a later section to help you do this.

Hopefully, at this stage, you will have begun to see the advantage of an intervention attempt. To be successful, however, you need a plan and it can be useful to consider guidelines which have proved valuable to others. Let us now outline some methods of approach.

PART
II

Intervention

The Intervention Plan

To succeed, an intervention plan needs to be appropriate to the circumstances of the family. In the discussion which follows we will outline a number of strategies which have value in making intervention a reality.

1. Nonenabling.
2. Consistent feedback.
3. Positive statement of concern.
4. Requests for action.
5. Refusal to be sidetracked by short-term improvements or promises to stop unaided.
6. Consistent emphasis on starting recovery rather than stopping the active dependency.
7. Use of leverage.
8. Constructive self-care.

Let us look at each in turn and evaluate its role in creating the conditions for intervention. However, we must recognize that it may take some time to achieve success. Persistence is required. You also will need to ensure that you are emotionally supported by friends or family while you are trying to reverse enabling and become intervention-oriented.

The content of the eight sections which follow is intended to guide you. In practice, you may find that some of the suggested strategies seem difficult to use in your circumstances or because of the way you feel at present. However, you will find a common theme as you read on — an active, purposeful approach to the problem of alcohol, drug or gambling abuse. This allows you to use your important role in the dependent person's life constructively, to break through denial and to create a sense of urgency about the need to seek help.

It is to be hoped that you will find some, or all, of the following suggestions helpful. If you decide to use them, do not be discouraged if they initially appear difficult to put into practice. The very changes that will occur in your way of thinking about the problem are helpful in themselves and, if necessary, you can seek professional help with intervention.

Intervention Strategy: Nonenabling

You will have gathered by now that becoming nonenabling is important, both to yourself and the troubled person. However, most families desperately want recovery. They need to believe that normality can be restored and there can be a better life in the future. If your dependent person is not yet in treatment, how, then, can you take nonenabling further and use it as an important tool in an intervention effort?

Nonenabling by concerned persons has some valuable effects, both within families and on the troubled individual. *The absence of behavior aimed at control achieves change in three areas.*

1. It increases the energy level of relatives and friends since they are no longer totally preoccupied with the extent of the dependent person's drinking, drug-taking or gambling. Newly available energy can be channeled into constructive self-care and improvement in

the quality of family life on a daily basis. These changes result in improved self-esteem and relationships between concerned persons. They also provide the rapport and mutual support which can sustain people emotionally while they attempt to intervene.

2. The absence of control by family and friends partially removes the basis for the dependent person's defensive protection of the mood-altering chemical or gambling experience. When control has stopped, blaming and rationalizations are no longer effective as explanations of ongoing use. The troubled individual is then forced to recognize compulsion and to accept that his life is out of control.

3. When friends and relatives stop controlling, the dependent person is free to use alcohol, drugs or gambling without restriction. Very often his condition deteriorates. Health becomes damaged and family and social crises become commonplace. These make the problem more conspicuous and increase his inner despair and fear. In these circumstances an offer of help is likely to become acceptable as time passes.

The absence of enabling behaviors aimed at protection achieves change in the following ways:

- Because nobody else resolves difficulties the dependent person is forced to face the crisis that arises as a consequence of alcohol, drug or gambling abuse. A crisis can be a turning point for the troubled individual because it creates anxiety. It also draws attention to the disordered lifestyle typically associated with an active dependency. In desperation or to avoid further problems the person in difficulty may agree to seek help.

- The absence of protection draws attention to the troubled individual's poor participation in family life. It also emphasizes his failure to perform satisfactorily in important life roles, such as those of spouse, parent, employee or work colleague. When relatives and friends become nonenabling, they no longer cover up inadequacies or take over the dependent person's functions at home or at work. He is, therefore, given the following messages by implication:

1. You have a part to play in the family or job situation that belongs only to you.
2. Nobody else will take over your roles and functions when you are absent, irresponsible or incapable.
3. Other people suffer unnecessarily because you fail to perform adequately.
4. You exclude yourself from family or work life by your repeated decision to give alcohol, drug-use or gambling first priority in your life.

A sense of isolation and failure are common feelings when a dependency is active. The acknowledgment and expression of such feelings indicate vulnerability and need and become more likely when relatives and friends have become nonenabling in this way. When an offer of help follows, a dependent person with these new insights is more likely to be receptive.

However, when concerned persons begin enabling reversal, it is important that the troubled individual is not simply subjected to a sudden change of tactics without explanation of their meaning. When you finally decide not to continue lying to an employer or not to offer further protection in a crisis, your new behavior may well be interpreted as rejection unless you supply reasons for your stance. Nonenabling based on anger which says, in effect, "You're on your own now," is not helpful.

Messages of the following type, delivered to the troubled person with concern, can usefully accompany nonenabling.

1. This problem has developed as a result of your continuing overuse of alcohol, drugs or gambling.
2. I am worried about the effect this is having on your behavior and our daily lives.
3. I cannot stop your continuing in this way, though I will be very happy if you decide to seek help with this problem.

4. I am refusing to manipulate for you or protect you further where your behavior has caused difficulties. I am not doing this to punish you or because I am angry but because these demands put me under an unacceptable level of personal pressure.
5. In saying *No* I am exercising my right to decide what is good for me and the family. We must survive and keep ourselves healthy and well, whatever you decide to do.
6. Naturally, for your sake and for ours, I wish you would choose to seek guidance and I have checked out the type of help that is available, should you decide to take that step.

Handling nonenabling in this way may seem something of a tall order. This is particularly true when the dependent person tends to be verbally or physically aggressive or when his behavior threatens the day-to-day survival of the household unit. However, in normal circumstances, family members have a right to live peacefully and safely. In some situations, a decision to withdraw from a seriously threatening living arrangement with an actively dependent person may be of considerable value in creating the conditions for intervention.

We have all heard the term *rock bottom* applied where a person has an alcohol, drug or gambling problem. For some rock bottom is a bottle of cheap wine in an alley. For others it is the serious recognition that the stability of family life or future employability is at stake. Many people seek help when they finally recognize that relatives and friends are no longer prepared to tolerate their dependency-related behavior. Ideally, however, the troubled individual facing this type of choice should also be aware that concerned persons believe there is something seriously wrong and are prepared to stand by him, should he decide to explore avenues to help him recover.

In reversing enabling it is important to undertake only as much as you feel able to manage. Your feelings also are important and you may need to pace yourself. You have a right to make personal decisions about the limits you set and the extent to which you choose to use inducements or leverage to stimulate change.

Some people begin with small things and move on from there. Others choose to tackle a major issue immediately. Whatever you decide, it is important that the process is started. When you undertake only what you feel capable of handling, you can be firm and purposeful. The dependent person notices this change in you and also hears you offering help. His own guilt, self-hatred and fear of the future may well do the rest. This is particularly likely if he realizes that you will not back down on decisions you have made and that you continue to set limits.

Living with the day-to-day stress of an active alcohol, drug or gambling problem, concerned persons can often feel "Things will always be this way." You can, however, initiate change by modifying your own behavior. Try as we might, none of us can force somebody to behave differently, against his will, without using an unacceptable level of coercion. But we can change ourselves and we can also influence the other person, particularly in a close relationship.

Reversing enabling, then, allows you to assert your own rights. It also stops the protection of the dependency which allows the condition to continue. It further helps you regain influence in the troubled person's life because he is now obliged to take your wishes and limits into account when he needs to drink, take drugs or gamble. This is particularly true if he wants his relationship with you to survive. He will gradually realize that he is compelled to give priority to alcohol, drugs or the gambling experience, even when it means hurting and disappointing the people he cares about. Eventually, he will come to recognize that he is out of control and cannot stop alone. At this point, he may become receptive to your request that he seek outside help.

Intervention Strategy: Consistent Feedback

Apart from explanations given by concerned persons for their new, nonenabling behavior there is another type of feedback which relatives and friends can give a troubled individual on a regular basis. This helps him build up an accurate picture of his unacceptable behavior and its impact on others. Such feedback provides a mirror-image for the person with the problem and allows him to see himself as reflected through the eyes of others. This is necessary because defensiveness and amnesic episodes create a lack of awareness of the severity of alcohol, drug or gambling-related events within the dependent person. He prefers to persist in the belief that, "There is no problem" or "You're all exaggerating."

Consistent feedback, then, is something concerned persons can start giving at the same time as they become nonenabling. *It centers on describing and stating the effects of the problem.*

This type of feedback has certain important characteristics:

1. **Nonjudgmental delivery:** An attitude of concern and a noncritical approach are vital.
2. **Appropriate timing:** It is pointless to give feedback when the dependent person is intoxicated as he may be unreceptive or easily angered or perhaps won't recall the conversation the next day. Ideally, feedback is given when the one hearing it is most likely to be receptive. Quite often early morning is a good time as the facts presented fill gaps arising from amnesic episodes. The troubled individual is also likely to be feeling remorse.
3. **Consistently given:** It is easy for the dependent person to brush aside the memory of feedback given on rare occasions. Because of the emotional changes occurring during the illness, the mind of the troubled person automatically buries unpleasant recollections that activate guilt and shame. Yet guilt and shame can induce people to seek help. Regular feedback can keep the facts alive for the dependent individual; his grasp of his problematic behavior will deepen over time. Eventually, shame, fear and anxiety become impossible to avoid. At this stage, they may motivate him to take constructive steps to help himself feel better.

4. **Personalized presentation:** Concerned persons who give feedback describe the effect of the troubled individual's behavior in terms of their own hurt, disappointment, anger, anxiety, shame and fear. They also underline the implications of these feelings for the short- or long-term future of the relationship.

As already stated, consistent feedback is focused on the description and effects of active dependency. Its themes include:

> *Facts.*
> *Failures.*
> *Feelings.*
> *Fears.*

Let us look at each of these in turn. While they are described separately here for purposes of clarity, it is assumed that several, or all, of the elements may be included in the content of any particular feedback.

In providing feedback it is helpful for relatives and friends to avoid terms like "alcoholic," "drug addict" or "gambling addict." They usually have negative connotations for the dependent person who feels, "I'm not that bad." It is often more useful to leave professional diagnosis and labeling of the problem to experts. They have the authority and resources to use their findings about the severity of the condition to emphasize the necessity to take further steps, if and when the troubled individual seeks outside help. Meanwhile, concerned persons can usefully refer to *problem* or *too much* drinking, drug-taking or gambling.

Facts

Specific, factual description of drinking, drug-taking or gambling-related behavior can be presented in a clearly detailed way. This allows the dependent person to imagine himself behaving as described, even if, due to an amnesic episode, he doesn't recall a particular incident. Content may include references to his physical appearance or expression and to inappropriate or abnormal behavior when intoxicated. It may also include statements about the specific implications of excessive drinking, drug-taking or gambling for the financial well-being or social position of the family. In a work environment data about job performance and long-term employability may be relevant.

In giving feedback of this type it is important for concerned persons to avoid generalizations. Statements beginning with "You always" or "You never" are not helpful — they simply create antagonism. What is required instead is reality-based material about intoxication, aggressiveness, embarrassing behavior or related financial and social problems. This is linked directly with alcohol or drug-intake or gambling-related artificial mood changes. The underlying message is that such behavior is uncharacteristic of the dependent person and would be unlikely to occur in a fully sober state. (As a dependency progresses, there is a tendency for irritability, hostility and unpleasant behavior to be expressed even when the person with the problem is technically sober. This puzzles and frightens family members. However, it is a classic symptom of progression, indicating that the disorder of mood has become well-established as a consequence of prolonged alcohol, drug or gambling abuse.) By the provision of feedback, the troubled individual is helped to see how far his behavior is deviating from normal and how worrying and unpleasant it is for others.

Failures

In giving feedback relatives and friends draw attention to the dependent person's failure to behave responsibly or to fulfill his functions within the role structure of the family or workplace. To avoid producing unnecessary anger, the term *failure* is not used. The message is, nevertheless, clear. The troubled individual is helped to recognize that his lack of participation and inadequate performance are creating disappointment and distress in people directly affected by him. He also sees how these interfere with the smooth running of the family or job environment and with the quality of daily life for others.

Where possible, it is made clear that the dependent person's involvement in these important areas of living continues to be welcome, provided he participates reliably and his performance is at an acceptable level. This type of approach by relatives and friends avoids shutting out the troubled individual. It indicates that he has a contribution to make within close relationships and in the family, friendship network and work unit. At this stage, the message is:

1. Your role or position is waiting for you. We would be glad to welcome you back as a fully functioning partner/parent/friend/employee.
2. At the moment, you seem unable to participate well because your drinking, drug-taking or gambling is interfering with your ability to live normally.
3. We would like you to seek help for this problem, so that you can again become the person you once were, both for your own sake and ours.
4. You should know that we are all suffering in the present situation and I'm not sure how much longer we can continue in this way.
5. We may have to consider some further steps in the future if things don't improve. However, it would be preferable if you made that unnecessary by seeking help now.

Feelings

When concerned persons give feedback, it is important that they express their emotions. The only feeling that is of limited value in this situation is anger. Intense, unfocused anger increases the defensiveness of the troubled individual and provides justification for counteraccusation and quarreling. Anger can usefully be expressed, however, when it is clearly linked with a specific incident. Then it can be seen as a genuine response, rather than an indication of a state of anger or hostility, which the dependent person will interpret as coldness or rejection.

In giving feedback the aim is to diminish barriers rather than raise them and it is hoped that concerned persons' genuine and understandable emotion will evoke a similar response in the dependent individual.

While appropriate emotion can add weight to the facts presented, it is important that relatives and friends do not force the issue by exaggeration or by pretending to feel when they don't. Some concerned persons eventually bury their emotions as a self-protective mechanism and may, therefore, seem detached and uninvolved. Most, however, feel grief, loss, regret, sadness, despair, anxiety, fear and anger to varying extents.

Genuinely felt emotion has intensity and depth and needs no explanation. If displayed at the right moment, it may well evoke a similar feeling response in the troubled person. When this happens, defensive barriers are lowered and a moment of accessibility occurs when the dependent individual becomes open to influence. He may then experience a resurgence of emotional closeness, which may encourage him to seek help because he recognizes the concern of others and the distress his behavior is causing.

Fears

Most concerned persons living close to someone with an active alcohol, drug or gambling problem are beset by fears; fear of the future, for the survival of the family, for the emotional welfare of children, for the dependent person's health. People may also be exposed to aggression and fear for their own safety or that of others. They may be afraid of personality changes in the troubled individual who begins to appear increasingly unrecognizable as the person they once knew and loved. Some people doubt their own ability to cope and, occasionally, such concerned persons fear breaking down altogether and becoming unable to function effectively.

Sometimes these anxieties are heightened when the stressful present is compared with dreams of former years. Then there was a future and the possibility of a normal life. Now grim reality has shattered hopes and, unless changed, the situation seems likely to deteriorate rather than improve.

Such fears are based on a genuine experience of ongoing loss or on real catastrophes which have already occurred or seem likely to happen in the future. They can usefully be expressed while giving feedback, particularly when presented in a specific way. Concrete fears about the physical safety of family members, financial security and the dependent person's long-term employability are factually based. So, also, is concern about damage to health arising from ongoing alcohol or drug abuse. When relatives and friends express anxieties of this type, they are giving a message of concern to the dependent person about real events and possibilities and emphasizing the risk of further deterioration.

Other fears are less tangible and center on emotional damage within relationships and on undesirable changes in the characteristics and personality of the troubled individual. These include increased self-centeredness, unreliability, irritability or aggressiveness. The expression of such fears can be valuable when relatives or friends are giving feedback, particularly when they can illustrate their anxieties about the present by referring to the dependent person's earlier hopes and aspirations for himself and his family or to traits and behavior patterns that were once an attractive part of his personality.

In handling feedback in this way, family members and friends remind the dependent person that he, too, once wished for a better quality of life and was a rewarding person to know before the need to drink, take drugs or gamble became central. This approach appeals to the side of the troubled individual which feels guilty and worried and also gives the message that there is a worthwhile person to salvage and restore if help is sought in time.

To summarize: Feedback about facts, failures, feelings and fears, delivered by relatives and friends in a concerned way at a time when the dependent person is likely to be receptive, can play an important role in helping the troubled individual recognize why he needs help.

Intervention Strategy: Positive Statement Of Concern

When alcohol, drug or gambling abuse causes problems, intervention-oriented family members or friends must adopt an attitude of concern. Concern needs to be conveyed to the troubled individual in an unmistakable way. Facial expression, tone of voice, as well as the content of the message delivered are important vehicles for transmission of the concern felt by interveners. We should clarify that concern should not be displayed as sugary sympathy. Sympathy is often interpreted as endorsement by the person with the problem. Real concern for another implies a commitment to contribute to the person's well-being. When dependency is the problem, family members or friends base concern on the firm belief that the troubled individual is in denial. It is understood that he is unlikely to recognize his need for help unless those involved make it necessary for him to do so.

Sometimes indirectly expressed concern is not enough because a defensive dependent person mistrusts or misinterprets it. We must remember that most people with a serious alcohol, drug or gambling problem are emotionally changed as the condition progresses. In particular, they feel suspicious of those close to them and view other people as a threat to their continuing use of mood-altering chemicals or gambling. At the same time, they often feel isolated and ashamed and may desperately want to break the vicious cycle of their dependency.

By expressing concern directly, family members and friends help the troubled individual understand that he is not alone unless he chooses to be. A positive statement of concern, coupled with a viable plan of campaign for recovery, can be a lifeline offering a path back to normality.

When family members and friends express concern for themselves, they help the dependent person recognize the emotional burden his continuing abuse is placing on others. In most troubled individuals this creates guilt and self-hatred. At the same time, those he is hurting are offering to help. He may find himself in conflict between his wish to please others and his inability to imagine life without chemicals or gambling.

The balance is often tipped in favor of seeking guidance by the turmoil of inner feelings typical of established dependency. Fear, desperation and remorse take their toll. Sometimes the tug of love is won because the troubled person finds the quality of his present life unbearable. The relentless drive to maintain a level of alcohol, drug or gambling abuse is eventually acknowledged as damaging to himself or others.

Sometimes, in the later stages of the condition, a dependent individual will cry out for help due to need and fear. Tragically for some, the appeal comes when family relationships, social position, employability and bodily health are destroyed. By active intervention and positive statements of concern, relatives and friends create the conditions in which the request for help can be expressed at an earlier stage. It is important to recognize, however, that the appeal is rarely direct or particularly clear. Even when the dependent person's defenses are sufficiently lowered to permit acknowledgment of his anxiety and loss of control, he will still find it difficult to capitulate totally. Therefore, agreement to seek help may be expressed angrily or in a guarded way. "Okay! Okay! I'll go where you want. I hope that keeps you satisfied" or "All right, I'll go but I'm not committing myself to anything."

The troubled individual can also change his mind rapidly, agreeing one day and refusing the next. For this reason, it is vital that concerned persons respond immediately when the cry for help comes. It also is important to follow through quickly with an appointment for medical or professional assessment. Those working in the field are well used to ambivalence and understand that denial and defensiveness are part of the condition. They also are trained to handle a consultation in a manner which, hopefully, proves productive in taking recovery further.

Intervention Strategy: Requests For Action

Prior to recovery, an actively dependent person cannot imagine becoming alcohol, drug or gambling-free forever.

Neither can he revert, unaided, to his former personality or behavior patterns. While still immersed in regular abuse, change seems threatening and impossible. Therefore, it is important that any request by others that he seek help is presented as reasonable.

The dependent person is asked to commit himself to getting professional guidance about the severity of the problem. He also is requested to accept advice about the steps he can take to restore bodily and emotional health. This request is reasonable and frequently repeated.

At the same time, family members and friends use feedback consistently to provide the troubled individual with an overview of his behavior. Eventually a point is reached where he agrees to seek help, if only to get peace. A constructive attitude is ideal but unusual -- anger and resentment are more common.

Many dependent people adopt and maintain an attitude of resistance when facing an assessment interview. Whatever the eventual outcome, there are valuable gains to be made. The person with the problem is alerted to the existence and implications of dependency. He also is made aware of the availability of help. Should he refuse to cooperate with recommendations, relatives and friends can justifiably feel they have done their best. If the situation deteriorates further, concerned persons can protect their own interests knowing the intervention attempt will have some positive outcome -- even if delayed.

The assessment interview itself can have a motivating effect on the person with the problem. It is useful in several ways. It clarifies the extent and repercussions of alcohol, drug or gambling use. It establishes a diagnosis of dependency, when appropriate. It outlines the services available to both the dependent person and the family. And finally, it encourages exploration of the troubled individual's willingness to accept further help. Some people, undoubtedly, need residential treatment. This recommendation is usually more readily accepted when presented by assessment staff. They can evaluate the appropriateness of their program in the light of difficulties that emerge in the session. When residential treatment seems unnecessary, alternatives such as outpatient services, personal counseling or participation in self-help groups can usefully be discussed. Assessment staff are trained to help create commitment and transform it into a concrete plan for the immediate future of the dependent person.

Intervention Strategy: No Sidetracks

The road to dependency is littered with broken promises. At certain stages, family members and friends extract them frantically and find their optimism turning to ashes time after time. Some dependent people keep promises to stop for a while but are unable to maintain prolonged abstinence. A sense of deprivation (based on compulsion) makes them so agitated and irritable that relatives and friends find them easier to live with while drinking, using drugs or gambling. Some have a *bout* or *binge* pattern but always lapse again. Usually, as time passes, the bouts get closer together.

Most dependent people feel beleaguered. Their world seems full of interfering people who won't leave them in peace — who want to take away what they most value and need — alcohol, drugs or gambling. Now and again, to gain breathing space, they stop for a while. Their abused bodies get an opportunity to recuperate and their finances a chance to recover. However, they look forward to resuming again when the heat is off. Meanwhile, concerned persons are lulled into a false sense of security. They begin to believe, "Our troubles are over" or "He can stop when he wants to." Unfortunately dependency is not like that. When fully developed, mental preoccupation and the urge to use are very much alive, even in somebody who is temporarily abstinent. With help of the right type compulsion is quelled.

In becoming intervention-oriented, it is assumed that relatives and friends are weary of promises. They also are presumed to have lost faith in the dependent person's ability to stop unaided.

Under the pressure of consistent feedback (which may arouse guilt and shame), some troubled individuals will temporarily change their behavior. They may also make an attempt to control or stop their intake. However, at this stage, such apparent improvement requires a major effort. The emotional aspect of the illness, if not tackled effectively, will make long-term recovery unlikely. Outside help is required to give the dependent person the relief and peace of mind he badly needs.

Having taken the trouble to intervene constructively relatives and friends serve their own interests and those of the dependent person by firmly emphasizing the necessity for a professional assessment. In any event, it is unsafe for an alcohol or drug abuser to stop without medical supervision. Withdrawal symptoms may occur with potentially serious physical consequences.

Intervention Strategy: Emphasis On Recovery

To a concerned person living with an active problem it soon becomes obvious that the troubled individual cannot afford to continue to drink, take drugs or gamble. The associated problems represent too high a price. Abstinence soon seems the desirable goal. Some relatives and friends express this demand during discussions with the dependent person. However, at this stage of intervention, the presentation of this idea in bald terms may be extremely off-putting for the troubled individual. He imagines a sober life to be bleak and meaningless. It can be far more productive for family and friends to refer to getting help, restoring health or getting back to normal. This is particularly true if there is reason to believe that the dependent person feels deprived at the prospect of recovery.

It is vital to understand that recognition and acceptance of the problem comes gradually. The initial participation of most troubled individuals in a treatment program or a self-help group is very tentative. As time passes, a combination of education, feedback, support and therapeutic guidance begin to take effect. They deepen the dependent person's awareness of the extent and long-term implications of his problem. In addition, satisfying new relationships and improved physical health create a renewed sense of well-being. As the weeks slip by the troubled individual begins to find recovery rewarding. Eventually, when the dependency is fully accepted, relief replaces deprivation. Now the newly recovering person feels glad to be free of compulsion. He also is grateful to have an opportunity to live normally and to compensate for past hurts.

Recovery is a step-by-step process to which family members, friends, professionals and self-help groups contribute. However, the dependent person is the central figure. He must, over time, accept responsibility for his illness. He needs to recognize that he now has a choice for the future. He also needs to receive support while struggling to restore normality to his thinking and daily life. It is necessary that he become willing to make effective use of any services offered. The fellowships of Alcoholics Anonymous, Narcotics Anonymous or Gamblers Anonymous have a particular contribution to make to recovery.

At the intervention stage, the above changes seem impossible from the vantage point of the dependent person. For this reason, relatives and friends may need to accept real limitations. Their most useful initial contribution is to help him get started on a process of recovery. If things go well, this will become more firmly established and valued as time goes by.

Intervention Strategy: The Use Of Leverage

Throughout our discussion we have emphasized the concern of family members or friends as a vital element to stimulate the dependent person to respond constructively to an intervention effort. However, there are occasions when an attitude of concern can usefully be supplemented by leverage. This is especially true where concern alone is proving ineffective in creating a commitment to seek help.

Leverage involves the deliberate use of pressure, either from outside or within the family. It is employed to oblige the dependent person to take account of the realistic demands and needs of other people.

Concerned persons may use leverage in an inactive way by refusing to protect the troubled individual from the sanctions of outsiders. In such circumstances the momentum created by the demands of others operates as an agent of change. This process forces the troubled individual to take his difficulties seriously. In certain circumstances a spouse, friend or other family member may choose to generate leverage from within. This is accomplished by setting limits or outlining terms for the survival of the relationship or by using the legal system to protect rights.

Some family members or friends dislike the idea of placing pressure on the dependent person. This position is understandable. Often concern alone is effective as an intervention strategy. When the troubled individual is slow to respond, the use of leverage can further his awareness of the need to seek help. Later we shall discuss circumstances in which concerned persons may choose to use a valued relationship with the dependent person as a lever. However, let us first examine the inactive use of pressure from others.

Crises are excellent intervention points. The troubled individual becomes anxious. These circumstances provide family members and friends with an opportunity to use leverage to create a commitment to seek help. By being nonenabling during a crisis, concerned persons leave responsibility for resolving the problem where it belongs — with the problem drinker, drug-taker or gambler.

While still enabling, most family members deal automatically with problems posed by the realistic demands or sanctions of outsiders. They pay bills, use contacts to forestall legal difficulties and cover up with employers. They also try to placate people who have lost money or been treated aggressively by the dependent person. While relatives and friends handle problems, the anxiety level of the drinker, drug-taker or gambler decreases. He feels relieved to be off the hook and will usually make fervent promises to avoid such difficulties in the future. He generally learns little from this experience. His goal is to gain a reprieve.

Soon, despite promises, he will forget the urgency and
anxiety of the crisis and rationalize his role in creating it.
Drinking, drug-taking or gambling continues until a further
problem erupts.

While resolving the next difficulty, family members and
friends become increasingly angry with the dependent person. They resent being forced to face unpleasant situations
they did not create. They are burdened, shouldering responsibilities beyond their resources and are usually uncomfortable lying and manipulating. As time passes, they become
increasingly implicated in the disordered lifestyle of the
dependent person. They eventually feel obliged to continue
to protect and cover up. Problems spiral out of control as
the troubled individual feels increasingly sure of the backing
of others. More and more risks are taken. At some point
relatives and friends collapse or withdraw under the strain.
Sooner or later reality catches up. Money owed and unpaid
can result in imprisonment. So can habitual drunk driving,
drug-related charges or physical assault. Mortgages can be
reclaimed, tenants evicted and household furniture repos-
sessed. Eventually jobs can be lost. In such circumstances,
families face ruin and the prospect of the disintegration of
the household unit.

Some dependent people agree to seek help only when the
final blow has fallen. By then, relatives and friends are too
hurt or disillusioned to care. When alcohol, drug or gambling dependency is active, concerned persons can learn to
deal with crises in a consistent way. This stops the troubled
individual from taking his eventual rescue by others for
granted. It also maximizes the chance of early intervention.

Alcohol, drug or gambling-related crises can be either
spontaneous or planned.

Spontaneous Crises

Many spontaneous crises originate outside the family unit.
Difficulties with the law, with employers, with financial
institutions or with aggrieved individuals eventually intrude
on family life. These create serious problems for concerned

persons. Though unwelcome, when out in the open they can be handled in a way which furthers an intervention effort. Nonenabling family members and friends can usefully make the following response to such crises:

1. *Your drinking, drug-use or gambling has created this problem and now has endangered you and the family unit.*
2. *This difficulty has arisen because you continue to drink, take drugs or gamble, despite the fact that you are now out of your league financially/in danger of losing your job/in difficulty with the law.*
3. *If you were functioning normally, we could afford to meet our bills/you would keep your job/you wouldn't have legal problems.*
4. *The present crisis is your responsibility. It won't help in the long run if I take care of it for you. Soon there'll be further problems because you now appear to be unable to control your drinking, drug-taking or gambling.*
5. *I feel you need guidance. I will support you in any way I can if you decide to do something constructive. I want us to get back to normal living. However, this seems impossible while you continue in this way. It would relieve us all greatly if you would agree to seek help. Please think it over.*

This approach takes courage and commitment to the goals of intervention. It escalates rather than defuses the crisis. In the short term it appears to increase the risk of catastrophe, homelessness or unemployment. However, by handling crises originating from outside in a way which makes intervention successful, it is possible to prevent long-term distress for the family. Financial institutions, courts or employers often are willing to consider circumstances. This is particularly true when they receive an approach from a dependent person who wishes to recover or has already sought treatment. When the illness is under control and sobriety established, the troubled individual can be encouraged to become responsible for making reasonable agreements and commitments. In this way, those he has wronged during the active dependency are eventually compensated. As time passes, normality can be restored and the family re-established as a stable unit.

Spontaneous crises may also arise within the family or in the households of friends. They usually follow unacceptable alcohol, drug or gambling-related behavior. Before becoming aware of the option of intervention, some families are seriously disrupted by recurring internal crises.

For example, verbal or physical aggression can create upset or occasionally injury. Irritability, moodiness or demanding behavior by the dependent person generates tension and anxiety. Behavior changes as those affected become withdrawn, quarrelsome, demanding or clinging. In some families there are battles and alliances, with members forced to make choices and take sides. The household becomes a vortex of emotion. While people feel caught up in the issues, they also are deeply insecure about the stability of the family. As time goes by, they become habituated to crises and quarrels. Sometimes they eventually relinquish normal needs for security and order.

Keeping The Secret

In other circumstances, recurring crises evoke shame and fear. Often the family has two major concerns, — "Keep it secret" and "Keep the peace." Where the dependency becomes a family secret, an intolerable burden is placed on members. We have already considered the isolation that results. Children, in particular, feel ashamed of the family and are aware that something is different or wrong. They become guarded or preoccupied and learn to avoid inadvertent self-revelation. Trust is diminished. Depression and loneliness can be common. Where peace-keeping is the important consideration, a spouse or child may be forced to act as a buffer to prevent disharmony. Quarrels about the dependency are viewed as potentially explosive. Considerable energy is expended maintaining a semblance of order and cohesion. Sometimes the troubled individual is categorized as "sick," "overworked" or "short-tempered." Others are expected to accommodate his needs. In such families, direct communication becomes difficult. Realistically based feelings of anger, sadness and distress among members are threatening and unacceptable. Unexpressed emotions are eventually buried and are transformed into resentment and hostility. While trying to function normally, family members in such circumstances usually experience hopelessness and dread of the future.

As we can see, the crises created by an active dependency result over time in serious deterioration in the functioning of the family as a unit. They also may create emotional distress and behavioral problems in members. While some family crises are not directly related to the alcohol, drug or gambling abuse, those which occur for other reasons usually are poorly handled by the dependent person. His defensiveness, detachment and self-absorption alienate family members who need support and expect constructive action.

Can crises, occurring spontaneously within a family, contribute in any way to intervention? The answer is yes — provided they are handled in a way which increases the dependent person's awareness of his disruptive alcohol, drug or gambling-related behavior.

At this point, it may be useful to examine some situations which are likely to generate a family crisis when a dependency is active. Most center on the following areas:

- *Conflict*
- *Aggression*
- *Disordered behavior*
- *Absenteeism*

Conflict

Conflict may arise when insulting, embarrassing or thoughtless behavior by the dependent person evokes an angry, self-protective or rejecting response in others. In an attempt to hit back or assert rights, family members may find themselves fighting fire with fire. They, too, behave badly. Their response unintentionally provides the dependent person with an excellent basis for rationalization. He has no reason to feel remorseful about his behavior when others have given as good as they got. If confronted about causing disruption, he can counterattack quite realistically.

Where a crisis of this type occurs, family members unwittingly give the dependent person the power to dominate. His behavior has an impact because others inevitably respond. Their reaction deflects attention from the original occurrence and also leaves a residue of bad feeling for everyone. Conflict-based crises of this type are disruptive rather than productive. They have no value in an intervention effort because they are reciprocal. They sap energy and increase antagonism. They also foster the dependent person's defensive belief that anyone so put upon and abused at home deserves to drink, take drugs or gamble as an antidote.

How, then, can an intervention-oriented family handle conflict constructively? Prevention is best, where possible. The following rule of thumb applies: don't participate, don't retaliate. Under provocation this is easier said than done. It can be helpful to remember that most dependent people are engulfed by negative feelings. They burden these on others, particularly onto vulnerable family members. While unacceptable, this is a classic part of the emotional illness of dependency. By refusing to react to unreasonable or abusive behavior, family members force the dependent person to *own* his rage and aggression. Their refusal to respond as expected throws the troubled individual off balance. This underlines his role as initiator in creating the conditions for family conflict. While not necessarily verbally stated, the new behavior of spouse or children implies the following: "You're the only person here who is angry or demanding. What's making you feel so bad that you have to act in this unpleasant way?" Oddly enough, this is one of the few occasions during the intervention period when it is appropriate for the troubled individual to feel isolated by others. When sober, he can usefully be given feedback about his uncontrolled behavior and its implications.

In some families, conflict goes beyond quarreling or verbal disagreements and includes aggressive behavior. In working toward intervention, it is necessary to understand the circumstances in which this can occur. Useful coping strategies can then be selected.

Aggression

Spontaneous crises may arise in families as a result of unprovoked physical aggression. While disinhibited by the effect of alcohol, drugs or gambling, a dependent person will sometimes express rage and self-hatred by attacking vulnerable family members. Most spouses undergo a process of trial-and-error learning as they attempt to protect themselves and others from this recurring threat. Some retaliate initially, only to discover that the backlash is as frightening as the original abuse. Escape then becomes a priority.

While avoidance usually results in fewer injuries, frequent exposure to the trauma of aggression can leave emotional scars. These damage trust, undermine security and generate hatred and destructive fantasies in affected family members. Fearing the consequences of disclosure, spouses in this position tend to conceal the problem from outsiders. They are often reluctant to take advantage of the support and concern of others. They also may feel guilty, believing the dependent person when he asserts that they have provoked or deserved abuse of this type. They feel responsible for its occurrence. With the passage of time people subjected to aggression may become habituated to violence. They find themselves remaining indefinitely in a situation which is both physically and emotionally hazardous. More usually, however, a point is reached where the spouse has had enough. This may occur following a particularly frightening or dangerous episode. Alternatively, a shift may result when the balance of power has changed in the family. In such situations children have become physically mature and now offer a serious counterthreat to the dependent person.

Sometimes instead of being a passive victim of aggression a spouse may be an initiator or participant. A minor-

ity of family members find themselves venting tension
and frustration by being aggressive toward an unresponsive dependent person. When drunk or behaving badly, he
may be pummeled and verbally abused until finally al-
lowed to retire in disgrace. The frustration which creates
the need to hit out is understandable but this game of
crime and punishment serves as expiation for the person
with the problem. By passively submitting to physical
punishment, he exonerates himself from guilt about the
destructive effects of his drinking, drug-taking or gambling. As a consequence, he feels emotionally justified in
continuing to play bad boy.

Some spouses participate actively in aggressive episodes.
A physical exchange can release tension and give shortlived
personal satisfaction. However, there often is intense remorse
and embarrassment about the impact on children. The
emotional damage is considerable and, of course, the risk of
injury remains. In addition, retaliation by family members
allows the dependent person to rationalize his involvement.
He counterattacks by saying, "You're as bad as I am" or "You
started it." He has no reason to feel guilty as long as others
react in a similar way.

**Where a family is being physically threatened, the need to
intervene becomes urgent.** Aggression of any type is unpleasant but it can provide leverage when used constructively.

Ideally speaking, an intervention-oriented family will
avoid unnecessary aggression. In particular, members will
not initiate or participate in episodes of physical abuse.
Where incidents occur without provocation, they can usefully be discussed with a reliable outsider. A medical doctor
or the police can be helpful in providing an objective
record should the family decide to have recourse to the legal
system. The authority and sanctions implicit in the legal
process can provide a valuable external lever. This is particularly true where an enlightened judge or lawyer accepts
dependency as a compulsive condition.

Sometimes professionals are willing to work toward intervention with treatment presented as an option. This can be selected by the dependent person to forestall or defer the penalties prescribed by law for the alcohol, drug or gambling-related offense. For this strategy to have maximum impact it is vital that the troubled individual understands that penalties will be fully implemented if his recovery attempt is unsuccessful. While this type of leverage seldom creates a high level of personal motivation for recovery, a good treatment program will work to engage the dependent person. As time goes by, he will usually come to respect and value the benefits of abstinence.

Despite initially mixed motives, formerly aggressive individuals can improve considerably during treatment.

Experienced counseling staff can help the dependent person explore his motivation to dominate others. This may involve working through past learning or incidents which stimulated hostile impulses and behavior. These will often have contributed to an aggressive pattern of response in conflict situations. People who behave in this way usually have experienced aggression from others at some point. As dependency develops, the likelihood of overt aggression increases because of disinhibition. Some dependent people become caught in a vicious cycle of aggression and counteraggression. While drinking, drug-taking or gambling continues, they find it impossible to terminate this dysfunctional pattern.

Treatment centers with Family Programs use therapeutic techniques to encourage those affected by aggression to express their suffering and fear. The dependent person is, therefore, helped to understand and to accept the impact of his behavior within the family. Identification, support and involvement with others during treatment encourage the emergence of a more caring side of the troubled individual.

Commitment to recovery implies willingness to make amends to those who have been hurt. It also involves working constructively to change behavior and begin personal growth. Many treatment centers offer aftercare programs designed to support individuals and families in recovery. The goal is to help people establish better communication and more satisfying relationships. Aggressive behavior during active dependency can improve in recovery. However, the pace at which progress occurs may vary from person to person and is influenced by the quality of marital and family relationships, post-treatment.

Although subjected to unprovoked physical aggression, some families prefer not to use the legal system as a method of self-protection and an aid to intervention.

As an alternative, a spouse or other relative can choose to set limits relating to aggressive behavior within the family. If specific reactions are considered unacceptable, concerned persons can decide on the use of sanctions in the event of a recurrence. Most consider some of the following:

- Withdrawal of affection.
- Restriction of companionship.
- Discussion with outsiders or the extended family.
- Temporary separation.

The selection of an effective sanction is an individual matter for a spouse or family unit. Concerned persons are in the best position to assess which aspects of the relationship are valued by the troubled individual. They therefore know the areas in which loss or alarm is most likely to be felt by the person with the problem. The choice of sanction requires careful consideration. It is equally important that concerned persons are firmly committed to its implementation if necessary. Most relatives or friends make empty threats under pressure at some time or another. Statements are made on impulse or action is promised. Then when the crisis is over, the *status quo* is resumed.

Given the desperation people can feel when a dependency is active, this process is understandable. It is, however, ineffective as a method of inducing change in the dependent person's behavior. He becomes habituated to threats and quickly learns to manipulate to make them unworkable.

An intervention-oriented family may find it valuable to handle unacceptable behavior in the following way:

1. When sober, the dependent person is given feedback about the destructive impact of his aggressive behavior on the family. This is linked directly with his drinking, drug-taking or gambling (though, at a certain stage in dependency, some people are equally aggressive when not actively using chemicals).
2. Concerned persons make it clear that this behavior is unacceptable and will not be tolerated further.
3. The spouse or relatives and friends outline the specific steps they will take in the event of a recurrence.
4. Should the problem arise again, the interveners make a point of following through to the letter. They behave exactly as promised and if challenged by the dependent person, they restate the original agreement.
5. When appropriate, they indicate that a return to normality is conditional on the dependent person's seeking help with his alcohol, drug or gambling problem.

I imagine some readers are now saying, "You certainly don't know my spouse! I'd really be in trouble if I did something like that." Well, perhaps you would. In some circumstances an attempt at constructive confrontation of aggressive behavior escalates the problem dramatically.

Where family members feel physically threatened to this extent, it may be preferable to consider alternatives. Sometimes the use of the legal system or the involvement of authoritative outsiders can further intervene. A certificate of marriage confers privileges but not the right to assault. Neither do helpless children benefit from continuing aggression.

As already stated, dependency can be treated. Any person with this condition deserves an opportunity to recover. However, if intervention efforts persistently fail, a family whose well-being is constantly threatened may need to give primary consideration to self-protection.

In some families aggressive behavior is more uncomfortable and frightening than seriously threatening. In these circumstances, the use of limits and sanctions may have considerable value. They increase the dependent person's awareness of the negative impact of his behavior on others. They also create urgency about the need to deal construc- tively with the problem.

It is necessary to consider several related issues separately. In practice it is assumed that the use of leverage, where valid, is complemented by the intervention strategies already outlined. The dependent person becomes aware of the con- cerned and purposeful approach of family members and friends. The introduction of levers or sanctions represents a last resort for some families. For their own peace of mind and safety, others need to set limits on the dependent person's behavior throughout the intervention effort. Their intention is to underline the troubled individual's deviation from acceptable standards of conduct within the family.

We are still discussing methods of using crises, occurring spontaneously within the family, as intervention tools. As we have seen, constructive handling of conflict or aggression usually require a behavioral change in family members.

Disordered Behavior And Absenteeism

Earlier we mentioned two other typical situations which generate family crises where a dependency is active — disordered behavior and absenteeism.

In both instances the dependent person creates distress for others, either by behaving in an unacceptable way when present or by repeated absence when needed or expected. Disordered behavior usually occurs when the dependent person is out of control under the influence of chemicals or the experience of gambling. By being clumsy, foolhardy or careless he may put the safety of others at risk. Apart from realistic self-protection at the time, the most effective way to handle this type of behavior is to give feedback later. Similarly, repeated absences or tardiness can disrupt a fam- ily schedule and create a sense of abandonment at times of crisis. Inadequate participation in family life can usefully be the subject of feedback.

Relatives and friends feel angry and resentful when a dependent person is behaving in either of the above ways. It certainly is tempting to have it out on the spot, as it temporarily relieves feelings of tension and frustration.

However, when intervention-oriented, a family will avoid unnecessary conflict.

It will try to use each new situation to increase the dependent person's acceptance of his need for help. Such crises provide a basis for feedback to the troubled individual from the people personally affected. A factual account of the incident and a description of its emotional aftermath can be given when the dependent person is sober. This procedure underlines the extent to which alcohol, drug or gambling-related behavior is creating problems for others. In the same way, the troubled individual can be told of the disappointment, anger and loneliness felt by spouse or children when left to handle important family issues without support. This type of feedback emphasizes the vacant role in the family arising from the dependent person's preoccupation with drinking, drug-taking or gambling. It also underlines the need for immediate action to deal appropriately with the problem.

Planned Crises

Up to now we have been talking of spontaneous crises. It also is possible to use *planned* crises as a method of increasing the pressure on the dependent person to seek help. The most usual crisis of this type centers on separation within a partnership or termination of a friendship or association. Some family members or friends of an actively dependent person find it necessary to evaluate the long-term future of the relationship. A serious review is particularly likely if the troubled individual remains unwilling to seek help. It also can occur when involvement with him is consistently distressing or personally unrewarding for concerned persons.

If protection of self or others from alcohol, drug or gambling-related aggression seems essential, a spouse may feel forced to take action to improve the quality of life. Even in less threatening circumstances, a continuing sense of being unappreciated and restricted can motivate relatives to explore alternative lifestyles. Their behavior is an assertion of the right to a more personally rewarding future.

Having reached some final decision, concerned persons create a crisis for the troubled individual by outlining newly formulated plans. In choosing to terminate an unworkable partnership with an actively dependent person a spouse is utilizing the element of loss as a lever.

Any decision to separate is important and requires careful consideration. For some spouses, it is never a real option, either for moral reasons or because of the difficulties involved in setting-up a viable second household. Sometimes separation occurs on a temporary basis — usually following a crisis arising from an aggressive episode. A spouse in this position can feel driven to leave in the interests of personal safety without necessarily wanting to terminate the partnership. On the strength of fervent promises to reform, many return to an unchanged situation. They often are forced to leave again when the problem inevitably recurs. A dependent person learns little of value from this type of seesaw behavior. He begins to discount separation as a serious possibility because each absence is short-lived. Alternatively, empty threats are made in the heat of an argument so he ignores them in the future.

An intervention-oriented spouse choosing to use separation as a lever needs to consider several issues. Is the separation conditional or final? How do I want my partner to respond? How will I feel if he does not react as anticipated? On what terms will I consider resuming the partnership? Can I cope alone if necessary?

Many dependent people have accepted help following the loss of family members or valued friends. Due to anger, disillusionment or weariness, some spouses separate on a permanent basis. After much soul-searching, they conclude that the relationship can never be viable. Sometimes they enter alternative partnerships and build a life apart from the dependent person. Quite often, however, the trauma of separation and loss motivate the troubled individual to deal constructively with his problem. Where recovery is of good quality, the relationship can often be reestablished successfully at a later date. With active dependency, the outlook for the future can be very favorable following successful treatment. Concerned persons ideally participate in the recovery process, so that accumulated negative feelings are expressed and resolved. This leaves family members emotionally free to begin again.

However, many separations are conditional rather than permanent. When other intervention efforts fail, separation is sometimes a final option. When a partner feels convinced that nothing less than *contented sobriety* is acceptable, it becomes possible to be firm. Neither promises to stop nor temporary improvement are sufficient to diminish the belief that steps must be taken to achieve lasting recovery. At the time of separation, the dependent person can be told clearly that restoration of the relationship is conditional on his taking the necessary steps to deal with his problem. In such circumstances, the leverage arising from the dependent person's loneliness and fear provides the impetus for successful intervention.

A spouse or friend committed to creating the conditions for recovery will present separation in a positive way. The option is chosen as a repudiation of an unmanageable alcohol, drug or gambling-based lifestyle, rather than a personal abandonment of the troubled individual.

To state, "I will reconsider our future when you've had help and are back to normal," indicates a constructive attitude. "I can't stand being with you, you have nothing to offer me" conveys rejection.

The first statement acknowledges the dependent person's potential for the future. The second categorizes and blames on the basis of the past. The difference lies in the acceptance or rejection of the concept of illness in relation to dependency. Informed partners or friends who believe that the troubled individual is out of control and behaving uncharacteristically will have the generosity to continue to care for the person behind the symptoms. They will also want to help him restore self-respect and regain his position in their lives. Their intervention-oriented actions provide the opportunity for recovery. It is in the dependent person's best interests to take it.

This leads us to another important issue in considering separation. However committed they are to the notion of recovery, an intervention-oriented relative or friend who uses leverage in this way must be prepared to lose. The dependent person may refuse to respond as hoped. Recovery can be induced but not forced.

In using separation as a lever, concerned persons have decided that whatever the outcome they are no longer choosing to live with an active dependency. They will also have made realistic plans for survival outside the relationship if necessary. While separation can be used as an intervention strategy, it is most appropriate when other methods are ineffective. It is best used when it has begun to seem a preferable alternative to living with the disruption of a continuing alcohol, drug or gambling dependency.

The core issue here for concerned persons is, "I want you to recover but I can't force you to do so. I have become damaged, too, while involved with this problem. I would like you to seek help for the sake of the life we could have if you were well again. However, I will not risk my own future or that of our children by continuing to stay with you as things stand at present. The choice about our future direction is yours."

This strategy usually produces immediate results. Most dependent people feel frightened at the prospect of being permanently apart from the family. To avoid loneliness and loss, they may agree to accept recommendations made during a professional assessment. However, if agreement is not forthcoming and the spouse implements separation, the troubled individual may accept help at a later date. This can seem small comfort to a partner who has undergone trauma and disruption, though it underlines an important truth about the intervention process. Any consistent, concerned attempt to persuade a dependent person to begin recovery will bear fruit, sooner or later. The illness is progressive and late-stage dependency is characterized by desperation, fear and isolation. The availability of help eventually becomes meaningful as difficulties mount for the troubled individual.

On occasion, despite a well-conducted intervention attempt by relatives and friends, the dependent person delays recovery for some time. By the time he is ready others have adjusted to separation. They may well feel, "It's too late now, he wouldn't make the effort when we asked him. He can handle it on his own at this stage." Even if a reconciliation in sobriety seems unlikely, it often is in the interests of family members to support and assist the recovery of a troubled individual. This is particularly true where children are involved because they gain access to a stable parent rather than one who is actively dependent. It also is easier for a separated spouse to reach reasonable agreements about family matters with someone who is sober.

By now I'm sure you're feeling discouraged. Earlier, intervention was presented as a new and hopeful strategy which would probably lead to recovery. Perhaps you were beginning to feel it was feasible for you. Now you may wonder if it's worth the trouble, particularly where the use of leverage is involved.

In our final section, we shall reconsider some factors involved in making the decision to attempt intervention. For the present, let us simply review the issues which arise when leverage is used.

The Use Of Leverage

When motivated to help, it can be disturbing for relatives to learn that a dependent person may need to be subjected to pressure before consenting to an assessment of the problem. Of course, this is not always true — sometimes concern alone is effective. Then relatives and friends are spared the stress of choosing to restrict the choices of the troubled individual, making recovery the only viable option. In deciding to further intervention by using leverage, it is essential that concerned persons resolve any misgivings they have. They must also feel certain of their readiness to follow through, if necessary.

As a dependency progresses, there usually is a gradual change in the way relatives and friends perceive the problem. As difficulties mount, a course of action which seems unthinkable at one stage appears necessary later. Many concerned persons become increasingly convinced of the need to set limits or make serious choices when other methods of intervention are proving ineffective.

With active dependency, intervention emerges as the only real alternative to ongoing misery for the family or a final abandonment of the troubled individual. When relatives and friends understand the illness and decide not to subject themselves further to its disruptive impact, they become willing to pursue a planned strategy to achieve change. Intervention undoubtedly takes courage and energy.

On the positive side, concerned persons can feel secure in the knowledge that intervention is now widely considered to be the correct course to follow when dependency is present. It offers the welcome prospect of success and the hope of recovery, followed by a return to normal living.

Improvement occurs in the majority of families who have become intervention-oriented.

This is particularly true where there is access to a good treatment program if needed. Even if the troubled individual refuses to respond to the lifeline offered, relatives and friends have genuinely tried to help. They can subsequently concentrate on improving *their* quality of life without guilt or a sense of failure. Joint participation in an intervention attempt helps families improve communication.

On the negative side, intervention involves sustained effort and a degree of risk-taking, particularly where leverage is involved. Sometimes concerned persons feel unequal to the task. "I don't want to make any further effort. I'm worn out with the whole business." A sense of weariness and apathy about the future are understandable responses to the long-term stresses of active dependency. Uncertainty, personal insecurity, fluctuating emotions and day-to-day upheaval are common. Family members feel forced to adapt and adjust, often to the point of immobilization.

Dependency creates turmoil; intervention generates change.

As a concerned person, you will find, on reflection, that you have survived to date by a process of enforced adaptability. Your lifestyle, personality, emotional functioning and vision of the future are affected. Your options are increasingly restricted by the central role of alcohol, drugs or gambling in the household. In other words, you *have* changed — but it was inadvertent rather than planned change and forced upon you rather than chosen. Relatives and friends of an actively dependent person are no strangers to change. In deciding to pursue intervention, they initiate rather than react and implement change in a positive way. Its force is employed to propel the dependent person toward a specialized source of help.

A commitment to change is an integral part of intervention. When strategies are planned and well executed, their impact becomes focused, purposeful and effective. Conditions are created in which fundamental change can occur — recovery.

Intervention Strategy: Constructive Self-Care

To sustain yourself while intervening, it is important to have support. It also is necessary to allow yourself the right to meet needs and to experience the normal, daily pleasures untroubled families take for granted. When closely associated with an active dependency, many concerned persons neglect themselves. Stress, isolation and preoccupation with enabling are emotionally exhausting. Sometimes individual freedom is restricted by the possessiveness of the person with the problem. Often the quality of family life is poor due to the secrecy required to hide the problem from outsiders. Participation in enjoyable activities may be impossible because of financial constraints or the unreliability of the troubled individual. Hobbies, family events and social life suffer. Relatives and friends may feel understimulated, lonely and frustrated.

For this reason, some concerned persons need to make a conscious decision to care for themselves in a constructive way. The aim is to reexperience satisfaction in personal, social or family life, even while the dependency remains active. This is particularly true if the troubled individual's attitude or behavior has undermined attempts to live normally in the past.

Even in the face of an active alcohol, drug or gambling problem, some relatives and friends continue to give realistic priority to personal needs. Others, however, experience difficulty in this area. Many need guidance to help them assert rights to normal, pleasurable activities and to good physical and emotional health.

For concerned persons who have lost the habit of self-care, it may be necessary to introduce daily practices which are personally fulfilling. These center on the following closely related areas:

1. Revitalizing self-worth and confidence.
2. Restoring physical health and well-being.
3. Reducing stress.
4. Establishing and maintaining satisfactory relationships.
5. Reintroducing predictability to daily life.

Revitalizing Self-Worth And Confidence

When living with active dependency, it is easy for concerned persons to develop symptoms of emotional distress and to experience deteriorating self-esteem. Dysfunctional patterns of behavior can also become established, contributing nothing to emotional health or problem-solving abilities.

As part of a policy of constructive self-care it is important for family members and friends to improve self-worth, while working toward intervention. Maintaining positive self-esteem and realistic but unrestrictive self-appraisal is a basic task of life for everyone. Involvement with active dependency usually impairs concerned persons' ability to deal effectively with this important aspect of human life. The period of intervention is a good time to begin work on revitalizing self-worth and confidence — knowing that the process can be continued during recovery.

Let us begin by exploring some of the classic ways an active dependency affects the emotional life and behavior patterns of concerned persons.

People who feel good about themselves usually display certain characteristics: they satisfy personal needs, respond emotionally in a balanced and appropriate way and engage in behavior which enhances self-esteem and effectively addresses the day-to-day difficulties and challenges of life. So a discussion of needs, emotions and behavior provides us with a starting point.

Physical Needs

These arise from basic requirements for the healthy maintenance of the human body and the expression of fundamental drives. They include the need for food, warmth, shelter and the expression of sexuality. Financial deprivation arising during dependency can sometimes make it difficult or impossible for concerned persons to meet these needs consistently. Sexual contact may become distasteful or be employed manipulatively within the partnership. In this situation, sexuality may become a burden rather than a resource.

Safety Needs

These arise from a need to maintain the physical integrity of our bodies, i.e., by avoiding pain or harm and to experience emotional security. If aggressive behavior is associated with the active dependency, threat of or actual bodily harm may leave safety needs unmet. Similarly, continuing uncertainty and distress can undermine the emotional security of concerned persons.

Social Needs

These are linked to the bonding process which occurs in early life. The experience of receiving care from others activates needs for love, affection, friendship, self-disclosure, communication and physical contact with people. Many family members and friends of actively dependent people become socially isolated due to shame and embarrassment. They may also limit contacts due to the restricting and unjustified suspiciousness displayed by the troubled individual.

Besides lacking friendships and involvement in a network of social supports, immediate family members of a dependent person may suffer need deprivation. This can occur in relation to social needs that should appropriately be met within the context of the relationship with the troubled individual.

A spouse, for example, may rarely receive affection and love or communicate freely with a partner who is preoccupied with alcohol, drugs or gambling. Emotional closeness is frequently lost — sometimes because defensiveness and sensitivity to threat make the dependent person increasingly unreachable and invulnerable. Most spouses feel lonely and rejected to an extent which varies with circumstances.

Psychological Needs

These are linked with self-awareness and the social context of human life. They include needs for:

1. Personal identity.
2. Self-respect.
3. Social reinforcement.
4. Recuperation and enjoyment.
5. Self-development.

Personal Identity

Some cultures value the expression of individuality more highly than others. Within some groups it is assigned a negative value and viewed as threatening to the maintenance and continuity of the social system. Where a positive cultural emphasis is present, the achievement of a satisfactory sense of personal identity becomes the equivalent of a need.

When we consider the idea of personal identity in the abstract, we assume it includes some of the following elements: A sense of self as separate, unique and auton-omous, with the right to make independent decisions, seek personal fulfillment, utilize and develop talents and the ability to act assertively in pursuing our perceived best interests. To some extent, these ideas are a product of the emphasis on *self* which is very much part of modern life. Several factors contribute, positively or negatively, to the development of a sense of personal identity. These are:

1. Physical appearance.
2. Traits and personality.
3. Social skills.
4. Talents or capabilities.
5. Beliefs.
6. Self-confidence.

Physical Appearance

Obviously, this varies from person to person. There's not much to say about the variation, except to recognize that some people are lucky enough to be endowed with the bodily shape or features currently acknowledged as beautiful by cultural stereotypes. Our perception of our physical attractiveness may contribute to personal iden-tity, though for some people it is not especially significant. Beautiful or unattractive people can sometimes acquire traits which are limiting. The ability to attract without effort may occasionally contribute to a superficial or nonreciprocal approach to relationships. A sense of per-sonal unattractiveness may lead to avoidance or early withdrawal from social relationships and, finally, to relin-quishment of need.

When we feel loved and happy, we also feel attractive. If we believe ourselves to be accepted, warts and all, by the people important to us, blemishes and imperfections can lose their significance. Some spouses of actively de-pendent people neglect personal appearance for a time or experience unpleasant changes in body image due to loss of appetite, overeating, stress-induced physical changes or injury arising from aggression. Most, however, do not.

Although physical presentation can be impeccable, the sense of being lovable and loved is sometimes nonexistent.

Traits And Personality

Although remaining capable of spontaneity and personal growth to varying degrees, adults usually display characteristic patterns of behavior, intensity of response, modes of thinking and attitudes which can be observed in behavioral form by others. These individual properties contribute to or militate against the person's adjustment and social integration. Our personal identity is linked with the way we believe other people view us. It can also include the private side of personality — inner consciousness, thoughts, wishes, fantasies and memories that are shared only in a very intimate relationship or not at all.

For our purpose, it is not especially useful to think in terms of personality types, although some polar opposites have been identified. These refer to ongoing characteristics which appear stable over time.

We are all familiar with the *extrovert/introvert* distinction. The former is considered to be talkative, open and adventurous while the latter is considered to be silent, secretive and cautious.

Another distinction is made between the emotionally *stable* personality and the *unstable*. Stable personalities usually exhibit productivity, social competence, satisfying relationships, resistance to stress and positive self-evaluation. Unstable personalities may display intense anxiety, nervousness, poor quality relationships, limited or fluctuating productivity, excessive dependency on others when stressed and hypochondriacal symptoms. People who are unhappy or acutely distressed can manifest some or all of the latter difficulties for a while. That does not mean they should be labeled unstable. Coping responses can change and improve, as can life circumstances and the quality of relationships. Anxiety and tension also can subside, if problems are effectively resolved.

Personality traits are of interest to us, since it is not unusual for concerned persons to experience changes in personal attributes while living with dependency. Sometimes other people observe and comment on changes. Quite often personal recognition occurs at some point.

"I've changed, and I'm not sure I like the new me."

Remaining open to change is a life-enhancing, adaptive quality but the change to which we refer here is usually in a negative direction. It may involve the emergence of a trait the opposite to the one formerly displayed. It may indicate a maladaptive exaggeration of an existing characteristic.

For example, a valued combination of personal qualities such as kindness, warm-heartedness and responsiveness may be transformed into the opposite — coldness, detachment and insensitivity. An outgoing person may become retiring, an optimistic individual morose and apathetic, a courageous person self-pitying and a confident person indecisive.

When an existing quality becomes exaggerated in an unhealthy way, the following may occur: A formerly gentle patient individual becomes timid, withdrawn and compliant — though, as already stated, the opposite characteristics may also emerge, i.e., irritability, negativity or open hostility. A conscientious, responsible person may become anxiously obsessional or, as its opposite, careless and undependable.

If personality changes in response to unpleasant life events or demands (rather than as a matter of individual choice), anxiety may be experienced. Loss of consistency in patterns of behavior, traits displayed or thinking processes can be alarming or threatening — giving rise to fear of personality disintegration. At some point during active dependency, a closely involved concerned person may be assailed by the panicky feeling, "I'm going mad."

It is important for us to recognize that continuing exposure to active alcohol, drug or gambling dependency places a serious strain on the personal resources and coping abilities of people close by. It is to be expected that individual functioning will deteriorate for a time as the additional life-strain is handled. Concerned persons can be reassured by the knowledge that treatment facilities, self-support groups and professionals have a great deal of expertise, warmth and experience to offer while work is being done to reverse unpleasant changes.

Personality traits contribute to personal identity. Some of the characteristics we think of as attractive or good enhance the popularity, approachability and social functioning of the individual who displays them. Concerned persons who no longer like themselves and whose personal identity is adversely affected can take comfort. The damage is likely to be reversible — with appropriate help and good motivation for change.

Social Skills

We all know people who can fit in anywhere — who present themselves well and communicate with ease. They usually listen effectively and respond intuitively to the needs of others in a way which conveys interest and acknowledgment. Social skills can be improved at any time of life. The ease or difficulty we experience when presenting ourselves to others within a variety of settings and contexts can affect our sense of personal identity.

A self-conscious person may feel inferior or envious of others who communicate with greater ease. Mannerisms, speech patterns, posture or gestures can facilitate or hinder social exchange. A person whose posture or gestures signify hostility will be left alone. Someone whose body language conveys boredom may be avoided by a socially anxious person but approached by someone who feels the same way at a social gathering.

People who feel relaxed usually appear approachable and sociable. For some concerned persons meeting new people becomes an ordeal. Even coping with the social exchanges involved in family life or neighborliness becomes difficult as personal tension mounts and self-confidence wanes. The effort of trying to conceal the problem can be isolating in itself.

Some family members, particularly spouses, experience emotional overspill. Potentially enjoyable social contacts with close friends may eventually need to be used thera-peutically to gain support. The social self presented is that of someone needy and distressed. However willingly given and valued, the concern displayed by friends can make some spouses begin to consider themselves a burden on others as time passes. This can diminish self-esteem and make social participation stressful rather than relaxing. A concerned person's sense of personal identity can then begin to change and deteriorate.

Talents Or Capabilities

We are told we all have talents — some of which remain undiscovered throughout our lives. Our natural assets and abilities make a considerable contribution to personal iden-tity — particularly if we possess and use talents which are valued by the society in which we live. Some concerned persons develop skills and abilities fully, despite the impact of dependency. Others utilize assets to a limited extent or perhaps feel obliged, by financial constraints, to work in an area which offers little job satisfaction or potential for devel-opment. A very distressed spouse may feel incapable of summoning the concentration and application necessary to utilize talents to the full. Personal development and creative potential are eclipsed as day-to-day priority is assigned to the dependency and its demands.

People sometimes describe themselves as being "on hold," "suspended," "half-alive." Children who grow up with an active alcohol, drug or gambling problem may perform normally at school and work. They could, however, become overachievers, driving themselves to the limit of their abilities and energies in an unconscious attempt to compensate for the unhappiness of early family life. Others, of course, under-achieve. Poor concentration and school performance are often associated with tension and internal preoccupation. A child, chronically worried and upset by home life, may not do justice to natural abilities. A sense of inadequacy and inferiority follow rapidly, creating failure-oriented expectations which determine future performance in educational or vocational areas.

Beliefs

Beliefs structure our expectations of ourselves and others to an extent which varies from person to person. We can subscribe to beliefs only or attempt to implement them as a guide to day-to-day behavior. Contradictory beliefs can result in very different life choices, depending on the degree of conviction with which they are held and the importance assigned to them by the holder. For example, attitudes to and beliefs about people can determine behavior and expectations of self. Belief in values such as kindness, altruism or the growth potential of others could exercise considerable influence over occupational choice. So, too, could the belief, "It's a jungle out there — every man for himself."

Many people entering close relationships seek partners with similar beliefs. Most of us hold a number of core beliefs which must be shared if a relationship is to be viewed as viable. For example, fidelity within marriage can be highly valued by both partners and form a cornerstone of their mutual commitment. Conversely, a long-term relationship between a partner who believes in fidelity and one who doesn't could be fraught with tension.

We often express beliefs by using the term "should" — "Marriage *should* mean happiness," "Parents *should* spend time with their children," "Children *should* respect their parents," "True love *should* last forever."

Assumptions about how things ought to be can exercise considerable influence on our behavior and, certainly, on our expectations of other people. We feel disappointed, upset and angry if those surrounding us fail to meet our standards, particularly in family relationships and close friendships. We describe ourselves as "let down," "betrayed" or "hurt." Where attachments are deep or a commitment to a shared life has been made, this intense reaction is understandable. Any failure on the part of the other is a threat to our personal security.

Most concerned persons feel betrayed in a thousand ways by the drinking, drug-taking or gambling individual. Minor betrayals are commonplace, especially broken promises and forgotten commitments. In the broader sense, major disappointments occur in relation to roles — "I feel betrayed because he is not the father/partner/lover/provider/friend I expected him to be." The emotional anguish is intense and grief and loss dominate. The ideal, the dream, the might-have-beens echo poignantly as the day-to-day reality of life with dependency transforms "I know you will" into "Why can't you?"

Even love comes under attack. The assumptions we make about romantic love are many: It should offer warmth/acceptance/support/acknowledgment/security/fun/protection/sexual gratification, all in unlimited quantities. Whether realistic or otherwise, our expectations about love are important to us and a good deal of our energy is devoted to finding the context in which we can receive what we need. Some partners are happy together before symptoms of dependency begin to emerge. Whatever the extent of disruption occasioned by drinking, drug-taking or gambling, good times can be recalled. With the right guidance, effort can be directed to restoring normality because that which is valued was real at one time. In other relationships, a functioning partnership is never achieved because preoccupation with the dependency is present from the outset.

Important beliefs are dispelled slowly if life experience consistently disproves their veracity. We keep hoping to achieve our ideal before giving up in disillusionment if we fail. Many spouses of actively dependent people continue to believe in love, despite restricted opportunities to experience a reciprocal and satisfying relationship. Sometimes they consciously hate the troubled individual and his behavior but they still believe — in something. "Is it him I love or the image of love in my mind's eye?"

The human capacity for belief is considerable. The right to personal happiness is important to us all. The psychological tortures and grief experienced by both dependent and concerned persons create confusion in relation to beliefs and goals — "I'm not sure what I believe in anymore." When this happens, personal identity changes with the emergence of a shadowy self, lacking clarity of vision and optimism.

Self-Confidence

Self-confident people display a number of qualities. They think of themselves as competent and are reasonably free of self-doubt. They assess their abilities accurately most of the time and are willing to put themselves in previously untried situations when it is in their interests to do so. They are self-reinforcing but able to acknowledge any failure to perform effectively without serious damage to self-esteem. They feel at ease with personal appearance and self-presentation.

Self-confidence plays an important role in the development of personal identity. A person who lacks confidence may consistently underestimate abilities and avoid potentially beneficial tasks or life challenges due to fear of failure. In the initial stages of acquiring self-confidence, most people need reinforcement and support from others. Within a partnership or family situation approval can be particularly valued because of the emotional significance of the relationship. For the same reason, criticism or disparagement can be particularly hurtful when delivered by someone who is significant in our lives. In this respect, many concerned persons are vulnerable to deteriorating self-confidence. In his preoccupation with drinking, drug-taking or gambling, the person with the problem may fail to provide positive reinforcement, at best. At worst, he may undermine and attack in a hostile way to demolish a spouse or child's confidence.

We also lose confidence following significant or persistent failure experiences. As we have seen from our discussion of enabling, logical coping methods are doomed to failure when active dependency is the problem. Concerned persons' attempts to control and protect the troubled individual do not result in the cessation of drinking, drug-taking or gambling. Personal appeals are similarly unproductive. It is not surprising that family members and friends experience loss of confidence and a diminished sense of personal value. This, of course, affects personal identity in a negative way.

As we have seen, physical appearance, traits and personality, social skills, talents or capabilities, beliefs and self-confidence help shape our identity as individuals. People closely affected by active dependency are vulnerable in the areas mentioned and can suffer damage in terms of personal identity.

Psychological Need: Self-Respect

To maintain self-respect on a continuing basis, we need to achieve a balance between behavior and a system of values. We also need to conduct ourselves socially in a way which takes into account norms of appropriate behavior. Norms or codes of behavior are learned and reviewed throughout our lives, as we adjust to the changing social and cultural environments we encounter. We can feel embarrassed or ashamed when our behavior represents a serious breach of the social norms of any group with which we are involved. However, ongoing loss of self-respect is more likely to occur within the context of values. The acquisition of values begins early in life through the socialization process. The family unit, educational system, religious institutions and media usually contribute to a child's development to varying extents. The overall aim is to shape and support children's transition from self-focused needs and impulses to social awareness, so that other people can be assigned equal rights and respect. Early values are usually presented in an idealized form and are not always compatible with survival and self-protection in later life. A normal part of the adoption of an adult identity involves reviewing or challenging the values inculcated during development. Some are then discarded, while others are endorsed. Most people eventually select a core value system which will influence their behavior and style of life. The achievement of goals also motivates behavior, although sometimes goals are incompatible with value systems.

Routine behavior patterns and important choices will be monitored internally within the framework of norms and values which constitute each person's expectation of self. Behavior which is considered appropriate will "feel good" while inappropriate behavior will "feel bad." This common human experience indicates that our ability to self-evaluate and self-correct is influenced by our emotions. We learn to associate certain emotional states or transient feelings with breaches of behavioral norms or value systems such as shame, embarrassment, guilt, self-hatred.

It is well known that when emotions run high, there can be some element of loss of voluntary control over behavior. We all are liable to say and do things we subsequently regret when very angry. Many concerned persons experience problems of this type due to stress and the highly charged emotions arising during interaction with the dependent individual. A spouse who believes that children need a secure, harmonious home environment may feel guilt and shame following a heated argument which the children overheard.

We all fail to live up to our values, now and then. Nor do we always behave impeccably in every situation. An emotionally healthy individual can accommodate and forgive temporary lapses, both in self and others. The assumption is: Such behavior is unusual or out of character and will not readily be repeated without a reason. Tragically, family members and close friends of actively dependent people can find themselves behaving in a way which diminishes self-respect on a consistent basis. They may not only lose control of behavior, but may also feel forced to behave manipulatively or unethically in order to protect the person with the problem.

In addition, disordered, socially unacceptable behavior is repeatedly displayed by dependent people when intoxicated or in a self-engrossed or hostile frame of mind. Within the immediate family, such behavior is usually interpreted as a negative reflection on the family as a unit. A kind of collective guilt and embarrassment is felt which further reduces individual self-respect. "I felt humiliated when my parent/ spouse/child did or said X." The self-respect of concerned persons is often adversely affected by active dependency.

Psychological Need: Social Reinforcement

We all like to feel part of the social groups that are important in our lives. The need to belong, to fit in, to be positively regarded is strong and can motivate and determine behavior. Some people go to great lengths to be accepted and approved. Social pressure is known to be effective in inducing conformity or compliance with the requirements of a group. In some communities and cultures ostracism is practiced as an informal, though powerful, sanction. The expression of individuality is sometimes incompatible with the demands of a group, requiring the person to make a choice or compromise between belonging and self-expression.

Concerned persons sometimes assume they will be negatively reinforced or rejected by others if they disclose the facts of the dependency. Sometimes disclosure does result in rejection, particularly where in-laws are concerned. For the most part, however, people are receptive and sympathetic. A very positive outcome of disclosure can be expected when the self-support groups (Al-Anon/ Nar-Anon/Gamanon) or professional advice are utilized. A valuable social reinforcement field opens up as new relationships, based on empathy and identification, become available to family members and friends of the dependent person.

Before outside help is sought, however, the social reinforcements available to concerned persons can be limited. Assumptions about other people's attitudes and response to the problem can result in underutilization of existing relationships and avoidance of new contacts. Even when support is requested, the reinforcement provided by others may be unhelpful in terms of resolving the problem.

Few people know how to help effectively when active dependency is the issue. Advice about tactics and countermaneuvers or hostile disparagement of the troubled individual's behavior is of no lasting value. Due to high stress levels, concerned persons will often need personal contact that permits self-disclosure. Having accepted the support offered, they can sometimes feel subject to subtle social pressure to follow advice or take the steps suggested, irrespective of their contribution to intervention and recovery. Confusion and passivity are bedfellows and, on a temporary basis, it can seem easier to comply with suggestions or directions which are not actually geared toward resolving the problem in a helpful way. Because our need for acceptance by others is strong, we can find it difficult to say *no* under pressure or to choose a course of action which meets with the disapproval of significant people. A concerned person selecting intervention may occasionally have to defy family members who advocate separation and disengagement from the troubled individual.

In summary, ongoing social reinforcement is needed by family members and friends when a dependency is active. Within a social milieu or friendship network, warmth, affirmations and acceptance can greatly ease the burden carried by concerned persons. If guidance about intervention or recovery is required, a specialized source can offer greater clarity of direction and sustained reinforcement than can well-meaning people, who are poorly informed about dependency.

Psychological Need: Recuperation And Enjoyment

In order to work effectively and maintain psychological well-being, people need regular periods of rest and relaxation.

Sleep is essential, though the hours required vary from person-to-person since natural body rhythms and needs vary. Diet and our level of food intake also contribute to physical ease. To experience enjoyment and mental refreshment we need rest, relaxation and stimulation.

A physically active person with satisfying relationships and absorbing interests or hobbies, enjoying a challenging but emotionally rewarding job, should remain relatively stress-free. Day-to-day demands for increased concentration and optimal level of performance will certainly occur. However, the person quickly recognizes that more effort or output is required to cope effectively with complex or strenuous tasks. Mind and body then work in harmony, automatically providing the energy required. Afterwards rest, relaxation and exercise allow the body to renew itself on a daily basis, thereby avoiding a build-up of stress or tension.

Where, you may ask, are such paragons to be found? Not among the ranks of family members and close friends of actively dependent people, it seems. Remaining stress-free is extremely difficult for concerned persons. Most become too preoccupied and emotionally distressed to rest and relax effectively. How, then, do high stress levels develop?

In part they are associated with emotions. Involuntary arousal of bodily responses accompanies mood states. When an experience generates anxiety, both body and mind tell us what we feel. A dry mouth, sweaty palms, butterflies in the stomach are some of the typical physical symptoms that indicate anxiety. Powerful emotions such as fright or rage also trigger classic reactions within our bodies. The physiological response to acute stress prepares the body for an immediate reaction. Rapidly available energy can be utilized as the crisis is handled: How fast we can run when chased by a bull; how strong we are when a child is trapped.

The response we choose dissipates the energy released. After a time, the body returns to a quiescent or resting state. If circumstances activate emotions on a frequent or continuing basis, this bodily system may be chronically aroused. High levels of tension result, together with other symptoms which indicate stress. Physical ill health may eventually occur as may somatic illness. In the latter case, constant bodily arousal causes healthy organs to function inappropriately. The resultant symptoms resemble physical illness.

Chronic stress affects the mind and the emotions, as well as the body. It also affects behavior. Mood changes or unpleasant emotions are more likely to be experienced. Emotional exhaustion may eventually occur but in the interim, there is an increased likelihood of the occurrence of the following feeling states: depression, frustration, irritability, tension, loneliness, anxiety, panic and aggression. Behavior can be dominated by impulsive acting-out or emotional outbursts or can become routinized and inflexible. Forgetfulness, poor concentration and impaired decision-making also may occur.

During active dependency, family members and close friends of the dependent person are frequently exposed to situations that are clearly recognizable as stressful. If anything, their need for relaxation and recuperation is even more pronounced than that of a person living a less demanding life. Chronically high tension levels, ineffective tension-release mechanisms and continuing exposure to stressful situations can create overload. Apart from the bad feeling that accompanies this condition, the ability to experience enjoyment is impaired.

The naturally occurring highs or pleasures of life are both physically and emotionally based. Body contact, eating, sleeping, physical well-being and comfort are important sources of good feelings. So too are emotional closeness, joy, happiness, sexual satisfaction and the warm glow of self-respect and achievement. Concerned persons can find themselves losing the ability to feel good when they should. Their preoccupation with the dependency can become a central life issue, resulting in relegation of important personal needs for emotional and physical recuperation and relaxation.

Psychological Need: Self-Development

Self-development is basically about personal growth and the utilization of talents and intellectual capacity. It involves the development of understanding about life and relationships and the acquisition of coping skills. It also includes self-knowledge. For many concerned persons, self-development in the positive sense seems impossible while the dependency remains active. Intervention and recovery stimulate personal growth and permit a fundamental change in life circumstances. Under new conditions, self-development is facilitated.

Conclusion

In our discussion of physical safety, social and psychological needs, we have focused on the ways family members and friends of actively dependent people can suffer need deprivation. This is not inevitable but it is common. Ideally, concerned persons will work toward minimizing unnecessary distress and giving themselves the right to meet needs, insofar as possible, even while the dependency is active. The intervention phase is a positive starting point for the initiation of change in personal functioning and expectations.

Emotions And Defense Mechanisms

We have now examined needs and looked at some typical ways concerned persons can experience need deprivation. If needs are unmet on a continuing basis, it is possible to become stressed and depleted. We can, of course, decide to relinquish specific needs, if satisfaction is unattainable within the context of social life, relationships or values. However, family members or friends affected by active dependency are not voluntarily choosing to relinquish needs. In fact, a good deal of energy is expended trying to recreate conditions under which needs can again be met. As the illness progresses, the troubled individual becomes less capable of responding to the needs of others. As the disorder of dependency becomes increasingly unmanageable, family members are less likely to meet needs satisfactorily.

Apart from need deprivation, *emotional activation* also may occur. This term refers to the ongoing arousal of intense emotions which may eventually result in high levels of stress within concerned persons.

We all are aware that some emotions are more pleasurable to experience than others — we prefer joy to sorrow, peacefulness to anxiety, pride to shame. We like to feel good. Emotions ordinarily arise as a response to the behavior of other people and to real-life events or changes in circumstances. They also are stimulated by our internal needs, including the need to maintain an acceptable balance between standards of behavior and expectations of self. Emotional response can arise as a result of external events associated with people and situations or internal needs and self-appraisal.

Emotional normality is slightly different for each person and can also vary during periods of our lives. Our normal feeling state is more or less happy, depending on the demands placed on us by circumstances and our ability to fulfill our needs at that time. Frustration, conflict or problems in relationships can affect our mood in an unpleasant way. On the other hand, when our lives are in order, our mood is calm and happy. If strong emotions are aroused, we have a natural tendency to revert to our normal mood state when the crisis has passed.

Sudden injury to a child, for example, will often activate an intense emotional response in parents. Panic, fear and anxiety dominate, until the safety and well-being of the child are established. If the injury is slight and the child recovers quickly, the initial emotion subsides as everyone gets back to normal.

When severe trauma occurs, it can take longer for emotional recovery to begin. Dealing with bereavement takes time, particularly if a close relative dies or the loss necessitates major readjustment on a day-to-day basis. Intense emotion of short duration can be unsettling but manageable, particularly if the person has adequate tension-release mechanisms built in to the structure of daily life.

As already stated, not all emotions occur as a direct response to changed life events. Many are activated within the context of relationships as another person's behavior makes us feel good or bad, angry or reassured, peaceful or anxious. When we invest in people and make them significant in our lives, we also give them some dominion over our happiness and peace of mind. If our expectations of other people are not met, we respond by experiencing emotional pain. This motivates us to take steps to resolve difficulties and restore equilibrium within relationships.

Under normal circumstances emotions are an important element in our experience of ourselves and our relationships with others. Positive or pleasurable emotions feel good in themselves and are an important component of the bonding that occurs between people. When referring to emotions, we often think in terms of opposites. At the same time, we use language to indicate the degree of intensity with which an emotion is experienced.

For example, the terms irritation, antagonism and fury express the intensity of feelings of anger. It might be useful, at this point, to outline some of the common human emotions. They can be presented in pairs, with one group representing pleasurable feelings and the other, painful or potentially distressing emotional responses: love/hate; hope/despair; desire/revulsion; joy/sorrow; peacefulness/anxiety; pride/shame or guilt; contentment/dissatisfaction; courage/fear; calmness/excitement, shock or panic; trust/suspiciousness, jealousy or rejection.

As already stated, some concerned persons can become emotionally activated when living with dependency. Powerful, painful emotions are stimulated so frequently that the natural subsidence effect fails to occur. Feelings of rage, hatred, anger, guilt and shame become commonplace as the disorder associated with dependency escalates. Grief, sadness and loss underpin the more activating emotions, such as rage. When we are angry, we feel emotionally stirred up and have a strong impulse to raise our voices and expend energy in activity or movement. We usually express our feelings directly in the situation which gives rise to them. However, we may also mentally rehearse responses until we have planned our approach or calmed down enough to confront the problem in a direct way.

Angry feelings, then, activate us by generating energy which we utilize as we express them. If circumstances make us angry a great deal of the time, we become tense rather than temporarily energized. Then we begin to pay a personal price — discomfort, anxiety or tension which affect our mood. This often is the situation in which concerned persons find themselves.

Sadness, as an emotion, has a pervasive negative effect on well-being if it is intensely experienced or prolonged by circumstances. Family members or close friends of actively dependent people sometimes feel sad for years, while simultaneously experiencing other painful emotions. Happy times, good times, peaceful phases usually occur less frequently as the drinking, drug-taking or gambling gets out of control.

Defense Mechanisms

One of our methods of handling emotional pain and the demands of reality is the utilization of psychological defense mechanisms. This term is used to describe a number of observable mental maneuvers people automatically make to protect self-esteem when it is threatened. Defense mechanisms are not deliberately chosen by the person employing them but are used without conscious awareness.

In what circumstances do we use defense mechanisms?

Defenses can help us conceal unacceptable needs or motives from ourselves. They also can allow us to meet needs about which we feel guilty or ashamed in an indirect or covert way — thus preserving our self-esteem. Our defenses also help keep painful memories and feelings out of conscious awareness so that we can function without being haunted or overwhelmed. In addition, defense mechanisms help us cope with the demands of reality by allowing us to pace ourselves emotionally in our attempts to cope.

It is normal to use defense mechanisms. They serve many useful functions. They act as a personal filter between reality and the self. However, an emotionally healthy person eventually will face real issues or important unmet needs and will try to deal with reality. The defense mechanism of denial is often helpful to people surmounting difficulties in life. A suddenly bereaved person might unconsciously employ this defense to temporarily cushion the overwhelming pain associated with the loss. We all have felt empathy for someone whose initial response to sudden death is, "I don't believe it," and we have also seen the numb, dazed expression that accompanies the statement. However, most people face the reality of death and begin grieving after an interval. *In such a situation denial allows temporary avoidance of painful reality.*

Defenses become problematic when their use permits the person to deny reality on a continuing basis and, therefore, they fail to deal adequately with real life issues and demands. Sometimes, too, defenses can hide important parts of the self from the user so that the person's awareness of his or her needs or motives is limited. In addition, if defenses are used to keep painful feelings or memories buried indefinitely, the person's ability to be appropriately emotional in present relationships may be impaired.

In considering defense mechanisms here, we must, of necessity, keep our discussion as simple as possible. In reality, they can operate in a complicated way with one defense protecting another. For present purposes, however, we will refer only to the more usual defenses utilized by family members and friends of dependent people. As we now see, concerned persons, too, may become defensive when living with active alcohol, drug or gambling abuse. They use the same defense mechanisms as the troubled individual, though perhaps in a less rigid, all-pervasive way.

Both dependent and concerned persons can use defenses to deal with internally motivated threats to self-esteem like feelings of failure, shame or guilt. In common, too, they may also employ mechanisms of defense during interactions with other people. For example, blaming and attacking are common defensive ploys used by most alcohol, drug or gambling abusers at some time. By keeping others at a distance or emotionally cowed, the troubled individual is safe to keep using. A spouse who feels guilty about a partner's drug abuse may rationalize to others.

In active dependency defenses can be used by all parties, to maintain a facade of normality with outsiders, as well as to protect self-esteem from threat. And, of course, the dependent person is also using defenses to keep the extent of his compulsion and loss of control secret from his immediate family.

What then, are the most commonly utilized mechanisms of defense?

Denial

This may arise as a result of a threat presented by real-life situations or the behavior of other people. To protect ourselves, we can deny reality if it seems too unpleasant to face. Denial employed temporarily, can give the person an emotional rest before the problem is acknowledged directly and dealt with. If used on a longer term basis, it can result in problems of adaptation to changed life circumstances. Many concerned persons use denial, for a while, in the early days of the growing dependency. A few, however, persist in its use to the point where they become unable to see the problem clearly or recognize the need for outside help.

Rationalization

When we feel guilty about our behavior or motives or threatened by the probable response or actual comments of others, we may employ rationalization. In doing so, we provide ourselves and other people with logical motives or socially acceptable reasons for our behavior. Family members and friends of actively dependent people can employ rationalization to protect self-esteem: "I wouldn't be so irritable with the children, if he wasn't drinking so much" or "I feel guilty about the things I said but, after all, he did provoke me."

Intellectualization

To avoid anxiety when dealing with a situation which threatens us emotionally, we can distance ourselves from feelings by handling or discussing issues in an intellectual or abstract way. Some concerned persons use this defense when discussing the trauma of dependency with others. To avoid feeling hurt, angry, rejected or frightened, a spouse or other family member may describe painful events without allowing the accompanying emotion to surface. "I understand it is an illness and I really shouldn't feel angry or take it personally."

Suppression

This defense mechanism can be deliberately employed on a short-term basis as a method of self-control. We can choose to push aside painful memories, impulses or real-life issues temporarily, while we concentrate on another task or activity. When worried, for example, we are commonly encouraged to sleep on it and we can use suppression to reduce anxiety in order to relax sufficiently to get a good night's sleep. Suppression is a useful defense mechanism, provided we don't allow ourselves to avoid the problem. Concerned persons can sometimes feel so emotionally activated that the use of suppression seems impossible. As a consequence, the ability to rest and concentrate efficiently may be lost by family members or friends of actively dependent people.

Repression

This is a powerful defense mechanism which is employed completely outside our conscious awareness. Its purpose is to protect us from overwhelming emotions, painful memories or unacceptable impulses which threaten or hurt us too much to be consciously acknowledged.

If we use repression as a coping mechanism to deal with a traumatic event, we can repress the memory of the event or our feelings about it or both. For example, a concerned person who has been very badly frightened by aggressive behavior on the part of the troubled individual may unconsciously utilize repression as a coping mechanism. Conscious memory of the horrifying incident may be excluded from awareness, although feelings of distress and disturbed behavior are experienced. The actual memory of the frightening event becomes hazy or out of focus but the associated emotional pain remains. As an alternative, a concerned person could remember details of the frightening event with clarity but feel numb rather than actively distressed.

We all use repression, though the extent of its use varies from person to person. It is a necessary but heavy duty psychological defense. If employed on a continuing basis, it can result in an overall reduction in the intensity of all emotions. This can be a protection for the user in relation to painful feelings but it can also result in a reduced ability to acknowledge healthy needs or to feel pleasant emotions.

Extensive use of repression is isolating, largely because it distances the person from real needs, feelings and impulses. Painful emotions or memories have not actually gone away. Instead, they have been relegated to the background but continue to affect behavior patterns and emotional well-being. A concerned person who uses a great deal of repression as a coping mechanism may eventually feel numb, detached or empty and find limited satisfaction in the good experiences life offers.

Displacement

If feelings or impulses are unacceptable to us or their direct expression is likely to be threatening to our interests, we can employ the defense of displacement to reduce anxiety and tension.

A man who is angry with his boss and afraid to say so may abuse the dog as a way of venting his feelings. By using this defense, we can partially gratify our impulses or relieve powerful emotions by expressing them in an indirect way or through a safer channel. Sometimes feelings are expressed in relationships with people who are not responsible for the original discomfort. We speak of this process in terms of taking it out on someone else.

We also deal with feelings of aggression, for example, by breaking or destroying objects or by strenuous activity. Sometimes a spouse will displace feelings of anger onto a child in the family. In reality it is the behavior of the dependent person which generates the rage and aggression. Fear of retaliation stops the spouse from expressing feelings directly to the troubled individual. The anger, however,

needs some expression, so unconsciously a child is selected
as a target. Sometimes there is a physical resemblance
between the child chosen and the dependent person. Dis-
placed feelings can be expressed toward any child in a
family or, indeed, all children. The short-term relief of tension that displacement provides carries a price-tag for most
spouses if children are involved — guilt.

Projection

This defense protects us from recognizing our undesirable qualities or feelings by allowing us to attribute them
to other people in a way which is unrealistic. If we find
our own angry feelings difficult to acknowledge, we can
believe someone else is the angry one and act accordingly.
The use of projection results in unreasonable or distorted
perceptions and attitudes as well as invalid assessments of
other people.

While any or all of the above defense mechanisms can be
utilized by concerned persons, it is not uncommon to find
a particular cluster of defenses which are used frequently
by individuals. One person may employ a lot of denial and
rationalization, while another may rely heavily on repression
or projection. Some defenses are more easily recognized
and acknowledged than others. Concerned persons who
employ displacement, particularly in relation to the management of children, can often drop the defense quickly
when they understand the origin of their negative feelings.
It is a mistake to assume that defense mechanisms are bad
and must be dropped or, indeed, attacked by others. They
are an important component of a delicate balancing act
between reality, emotions, needs and self-concept. Their
function is to maintain psychological equilibrium. When
warmly supported and gently made aware of the defenses
being employed, most concerned persons become able to
acknowledge emotional pain and to assess their motives
and needs in a more realistic way. Professional help can be
invaluable in this regard.

So far we have looked at need deprivation, emotional activation, stress and psychological defense mechanisms. It may now be helpful to describe some typical spouse profiles to provide us with an understanding of the types of distress that may be experienced.

These profiles are intended for guidance only. There is no suggestion that an individual reader has to fit in to one category or another. In fact, many spouses don't belong clearly in any or alternatively display elements of all three.

The profiles are of:

The Agitated Spouse.
The Depleted Spouse.
The Composed Spouse.

The Agitated Spouse

A spouse in this position feels emotionally activated and experiences intense fluctuating reactions to each event of the dependency. The response represents the spouse's attempt to restore equilibrium within the family and to realign the relationship with the troubled individual so needs and expectations can be met.

Typical Statement:
"I care intensely."

Predominant Characteristic: Emotional Expression.
Emotions are activated, experienced and displayed in response to unpredictable situational cues. These arise in the context of the relationship with the troubled individual, as the active dependency increasingly affects the partnership and family life.

Recurrent Feelings:
Anger/resentment/outrage/grief/fear/self-pity.

Behavior Pattern:
Variable/trial-and-error behavior/high activity levels — "I'll try anything."

Predominant Attitude:

Active/corrective/assertive. The relationship is assumed to be restorable if the right tactics can be discovered and employed. Emotional expression and behavioral maneuvers are utilized by the spouse in an attempt to minimize and correct the disorder of dependency and to get the relationship back to normal.

Preoccupations Within The Partnership:

1. Predominance of control-based enabling, though any type may be utilized.
2. Frequent swings from retaliation to reconciliation.

Possible Features:

1. Intense preoccupation with day-to-day events. Immediate, openly displayed emotional reactions.
2. Powerful emotions dominate, i.e., anger/guilt/fear.
3. Emotions fluctuate between extremes, i.e., love/hate/hope/fear.
4. Frequent episodes of acute distress, i.e., crying.
5. Attitudinal postures emerge, i.e., hatred/blame.

Personal Defense System:

Defense mechanisms are beginning to be utilized but are mainly focused on denying or minimizing the implications of the dependency. Defenses to protect self-esteem arise, such as rationalizing and blaming but, as yet, the defense system is not sufficiently developed to protect the spouse from pervasive emotional distress. Suppression is utilized following intensely emotionally threatening episodes. Repression is not employed to any great extent though displacement of feelings may occur.

Adolescent Lament

Jenny: (to brother Tony) I don't understand either of them! Mom is always angry or upset these days. She's constantly fighting with Dad. She watches him all the time and picks on him for everything! She's furious with him for drinking. She seems to hate him, really . . . And then, sometimes, if he's nice to her, she acts as though she's happy — for a while. She's completely caught up with him. She can't talk about anything, except what he's doing now or did yesterday. She's irritable when I talk to her — especially if she thinks I'm criticizing her attitude to Dad. She keeps trying to involve me — to get me to take her side against him . . . Do you know what she did the other night? Mom had to go out and was afraid to leave Dad — she thought he'd drink. She wanted me to stay home — to "Dad-Sit," so to speak. I told her I'd planned to go to Carol's house but she just didn't let up! In the end I felt so guilty, I stayed. What an evening! The tension was terrible. I didn't know what to say to Dad and he knew very well he was being watched. It was humiliating for both of us . . . Oh, Tony, I'm glad you're home. Maybe you can do something, say something . . . The whole situation makes me feel terrible! I'm worried about them. Dad is drinking too much and Mom is pushing and nagging and watching all the time. They seem to be caught in this battle! I feel frightened, left out and yet drawn in . . . I'm so confused. I just don't understand.

Tony: But, Jenny, what you're saying seems incredible! I know I've been away two years but they always got on well before. Dad always drank. Mother didn't seem to mind then. What's so different now?

Jenny: Don't you understand? He's drinking more. He's out a lot. He doesn't come home when he says he will. Sometimes he's drunk. His speech is slurred and he can hardly stand. He's really out of it! I don't blame Mom for being worried but she's driving him to it the way she's behaving. Half the time she's on the warpath and whenever he's all right, we play *Happy Families*. I'm supposed to drop my friends and go out with them — just like that! Two months ago, Mom decided they needed a second honeymoon. What a disaster that was. They were back after two days. Apparently Dad never stopped drinking. They had some terrible fights and came home. Mom didn't speak to him for a month — though, really, she hardly got an opportunity since he was out most of the time. The whole situation is a mess, Tony. I don't know what to do. Anyway, at least you're here.

The Depleted Spouse

A spouse in this position feels highly stressed and emotionally exhausted. The effort of coping with the demands of dependency has become overwhelming and an attitude of avoidance predominates. The focus is on self-maintenance, tension management and comfort-seeking behavior.

Typical Statement:
"I feel too bad to care."

Predominant Characteristic:
Emotional containment and internalized distress. Emotions are experienced as personally depleting and their expression brings limited or no lasting relief.

Recurrent Feelings:
Depression/worthlessness/anxiety/hopelessness/fear/self-hatred.

Behavior Pattern:
Routinized/rigid — lacking versatility/energy-husbanded. "I can't be bothered," "It's too much effort."

Predominant Attitude:
Passive/unfocused. The spouse feels and is perceived by others as uncertain/helpless/apathetic/withdrawn.

Preoccupation Within The Partnership:

1. Avoidance of conflict or constructive confrontation.
2. Predominance of protection-based enabling as control-based methods may have been experienced as unproductive.

Possible Features:

1. The combination of prolonged emotional activation and need deprivation, coupled with the ongoing demands of dependency, create high levels of stress.

2. Exhaustion/fatigue: Sleep is employed as an avoidance mechanism which does not refresh or replenish energy.
3. Restlessness/high levels of tension/sleeplessness.
4. Loss of appetite or comfort eating.
5. Use of tranquilizers/sedatives/sleeping pills. Fear of a nervous breakdown.
6. Anhedonia: Loss of the ability to respond with enjoyment or to experience pleasure.
7. Palliative coping mechanisms used, such as excessive intake of food, alcohol, drugs, sleep.
8. Comfort-seeking impulsive behaviors, such as excessive spending.
9. Emotional sensitization/overintense reactivity to minor problems/irritability/moodiness.
10. Impaired judgment/poor concentration and decision-making/impaired short-term memory/loss of clarity of thought.
11. Rigidity/loss of reasonableness/versatility/new approaches avoided.
12. Blunted affect/heavy feeling/dull rather than acute emotional pain/crying may become difficult.
13. Relinquishment of social and emotional needs.
14. Somatic symptoms/ill health.

Personal Defense System:
Predominance of avoidance-based defense mechanisms such as denial, minimizing, suppression. Repression is being utilized to avoid unpleasant memories but it is not yet fully effective in protecting the spouse from emotional pain. Distress is still experienced though in a less acute form.

A New Day

It can't be time to get up already. I'm exhausted. I'd love to sleep and sleep. I can't face another day. I don't think I ever felt so bad. My mind feels full of cotton wool. I'm so tired. I wish I could go away — just pack a bag and leave everything. I can't even stand the children — they irritate me. And I used to enjoy them so much. I'm snappy all the time — I feel rotten about that . . . What am I going to do? I'm confused. I feel so alone. There's no one I can really talk to. How can I tell anybody what's happening to me when I don't understand it myself? I used to be so energetic! Now I just drag myself around. I don't seem to enjoy anything anymore. I'm eating too much as well — I've gained so much weight. I hate myself right now. And things are so bad between Brian and me. He hardly even talks to me anymore. He's spending so much money at the race-track. We're really in trouble. I'm afraid to think what's going to happen to us. I just don't want to face it. I wish I could go away — hide somewhere. I'd love to wake up one morning and find it's all a bad dream. Maybe I should see my doctor — but it's too much trouble to drag the children all the way over there. I even hate shopping now. Every little thing is an effort. What is the matter with me? I've got to pull myself together somehow.

The Composed Spouse

A spouse in this position feels emotionally empty at a conscious level but has considerable repressed emotional pain. The ability to feel intensely is limited, affecting both positive/ pleasurable emotions, as well as painful feelings. Conscious memory of emotionally distressing episodes in the past has been lost, resulting in hazy or veiled recollection of the more threatening or frightening events of the dependency. Emotionally-charged memories or unmet needs are put to the back of the mind. This defense system reduces internal conflict. Energies are devoted to reorganization of social, vocational and family life in order to exclude the dependent person or minimize the impact of his disordered behavior.

Typical Statement:
"I'm beyond caring."

Predominant Characteristic: Emotional Suppression.
Emotional responsiveness diminishes as defenses are increasingly employed as a coping mechanism.

Recurrent Feelings:
Numb/cold/detached/empty; feelings of hatred, indifference or revulsion toward the dependent person.

Behavior Pattern:

Active/assertive/exploratory/problem-solving with a particular commitment to personal and family survival. Reassertion of self as competent in the management and reorganization of day-to-day affairs — "It has to be done, and there's no one else to do it."

Predominant Attitude:

Implacability and self-sufficiency in relation to daily tasks. Disillusionment/unresponsiveness/indifference in relation to the dependent person.

Preoccupations Within The Partnership:

1. Delineation of boundaries.
2. Restructuring of roles and relationships.
3. Control-based enabling and/or compensating and correcting as protection strategies; all types of enabling may be utilized.
4. Separation or termination of the relationship may be seriously considered.

Possible Features:

1. Generalized loss of emotional responsiveness, which influences reaction to any life situation or emotional demand.
2. Relinquishment of emotional needs within the context of the partnership.
3. Firmly established negative attitudes toward the dependent person with boundaries erected to maintain emotional distance.
4. Revitalization of social life/activities outside the family.
5. Exterior display of competence conceals poor self-esteem and self-doubt.
6. Crying becomes difficult — "I can't be bothered to cry" or "I feel cried out."
7. The emotional distress of others (particularly children in the family) may be perceived as threatening, giving rise to superficial or inadequate responses.

8. Denial or avoidance of the dependent person's need for help.

Personal Defense System:
There is a well-developed defense system with considerable use of repression. Defenses function effectively to protect spouse from awareness of emotional pain but penalties include an overall loss of responsiveness and the development of a backlog of bad feelings.

Starting Over

Susan: Are you sure, Roberta? Do you really want to do this? It's a big step. Naturally, I'll help you any way I can — if you feel it's right for you. I just want you to be certain.

Roberta: I'm sure, Susan. I'm leaving him. I'm just not putting up with it anymore! He's had his chance. He's made more promises than I can remember — but he's still on drugs. I've had it. I've made up my mind and I'm not going to change it. He's on his own now. As far as I'm concerned, he can do what he likes from now on.

Susan: But shouldn't he get help, Roberta? Surely there's somewhere he could go? I mean . . . it's such a change to see you like this. You seem so determined — almost cold. It's as though this was happening to somebody else. You must be feeling terrible inside. You know you don't have to put on a brave face for me.

Roberta: Look, Susan . . . I spent years crying, feeling bad, wondering what was wrong with me. I'm not doing it anymore. I'm going to look after myself now. I have to! He's not going to do it — not that he ever did.

Susan: But in the beginning you seemed happy together. I thought . . .

Roberta: That was years ago. I haven't been happy for a long time. Let's not argue, Susan. I'm leaving. I'm not asking you to agree with me. Naturally, I'd like to believe we're still friends.

Susan: Oh, of course we are. It's just that I know Jim, too, and feel so sad about this . . . Could he get help, do you think? Should I try to find out?

Roberta: It's pointless! I don't know how many times I've suggested it to him. He's just not interested. He only thinks about himself. I don't count.

Susan: I'm sorry, Roberta. I can't help crying . . . It's such a shock. I feel so sad for both of you.

Roberta: Don't waste your tears on me, Susan. I'm grateful for your sympathy, but I'll survive. I have to.

Conclusion

Involvement with active dependency often makes a major impact on concerned persons from an emotional point of view. As already stated, painful, frightening or confusing experiences occur frequently, sometimes creating an ongoing state of emotional activation. Important psychological, social and safety needs may be consistently unmet or only partially gratified. Day-to-day dependency-related crises demand continuing adaptation and correction. It is hardly surprising that high levels of stress can develop. Psychological defense mechanisms are among the coping strategies which concerned persons use to maintain emotional equilibrium.

It is unusual to meet concerned persons, particularly spouses, who have not become emotionally distressed and need-deprived. Dependency is often described as a family illness, not because everybody has it but because everyone is affected by it. It is painful to feel bad on a consistent basis and family members and friends are often confused by their inner turmoil. It is frightening to feel out of control or overwhelmed or to become aware of unpleasant personality or behavior changes in oneself. The fear of a nervous breakdown or personal disintegration is common.

Perhaps, at this point, some of you feel discouraged. Possibly, while reading, you found yourself identifying your own unmet needs, painful feelings or habitual defense mechanisms. During bad periods in our lives, self-awareness can hurt because it forces us to acknowledge the distress we are experiencing. The overall purpose of this discussion is to alert you to the value of constructive self-care as an intervention strategy.

How then, you ask, is it possible to care for yourself while feeling bad?

The first step for intervention-oriented concerned persons is to acknowledge personal distress. The second step is to normalize it. Instead of feeling different or freakish or crazy, family members and friends need to accept that it is normal to feel bad in an abnormal situation. The very fact that powerful emotions and defensiveness are present indicate healthy self-protectiveness. Need deprivation has the same significance in that the pain of not having what we need alerts us to the presence of the need itself. Being able to acknowledge unmet needs and change aspects of our lives so that needs can be met is normal and healthy. Most concerned persons need outside help to feel well again. The self-support groups (Al-Anon, Nar-Anon, Gamanon) are an excellent starting point for most people. Professional help from a counselor or therapist specializing in dependency and intervention is also of considerable value.

It is vital for family members and friends to recognize that it can take some time to deal effectively with emotional distress. While working toward intervention, it is important to view constructive self-care as a strategy for the revitalization of self. It is possible to begin to feel good again, independently of the progress of the dependent person. This involves a process, a direction, rather than a one-off personal decision or therapeutic contact. It presupposes self-help as well as the utilization of all available resources. It represents a commitment to oneself — a choice. Initiating personal recovery eventually permits the renewal of all facets of the functioning of family members or friends. If the dependent person is professionally treated in a residential or outpatient program, participating concerned persons will have the opportunity to use therapeutic resources for personal growth work.

As we continue our discussion of constructive self-care, we will focus on strategies concerned persons can use to begin the process of personal recovery. We have already touched on many of these ideas. However, it may prove useful to provide some guidelines for change.

Restoring Physical Health And Well-Being

Dealing with active dependency is, at best, a challenge. At worst it is a major stress. To cope successfully, it is essential to feel well. Some concerned persons become exhausted due to sleeplessness or sleep disruption. Others lose or gain weight due to tension, restlessness or comfort eating. Anxiety states and depression are common. While tranquilizers or sleeping pills alleviate symptoms in the short-term, ongoing use creates difficulties. Dependency may occur and their use blurs the edges of reality, so that problem-solving is deferred.

Physical illness can occur as relatives develop symptoms which may well be stress-related such as stomach ulcers, chronic backache, headaches, hair loss, gastric upsets, skin ailments or chronic asthma. A minority are in constant poor health due to injury resulting from aggression or lack of nutrition due to financial deprivation.

What to do? If you feel generally unwell or ill in a specific way, try to see a doctor and discuss your situation frankly. Some concerned persons minimize problems even in the doctor's care. They also avoid seeking medical care following injury or ill-treatment because of fear or shame. Your doctor can be an ally when informed of your difficulties. In addition to guiding you back to good health, it is often possible to use a medical consultation with the dependent person as an intervention point. Where aggression occurs, a doctor's record of shock, injury or complications can provide material for a medical report. This could be invaluable should you ever need to take legal steps to protect your interests.

On the other hand, if you are simply worn out, try to rest, eat and sleep. How often have you sat, tensely waiting for the dependent person to come home, when you could have been relaxing or doing something enjoyable? When you understand enabling, you recognize that you have no control over the drinking, drug-taking or gambling. Then you can experience the freedom of mind to use waiting time or free time to care for yourself and restore your energies.

Reducing Stress

The term "stress" can refer both to the event with which we have to cope and to our own response while coping.

When we are feeling well and happy, we can cope successfully with incidents which might cause real distress if we
were tired or isolated. Similar events can make varying
levels of demand on us, depending on our frame of mind. So
our way of perceiving a stressful event is an important
element in our response. We are particularly likely to become
distressed when we are overloaded with too much to handle
at once or when we are understimulated, bored or routinized. We are also vulnerable when personal exhaustion or
past experience of failure in coping make us doubt our
competence to deal successfully with the current difficulty.

Our sense of ourselves as stressed originates in our minds,
insofar as our thinking controls our way of viewing the
problem. Of course, living with an active dependency is
undoubtedly stressful in itself. The very fact that it is widely
recognized as a family illness underlines this.

It is virtually impossible to live with problematic drinking,
drug-taking or gambling without becoming personally distressed at some level. While concerned persons have little
control over the disordered behavior of the dependent person, they can change their personal reaction to the problem.
They can also modify their evaluation of their own coping.

Adults, in particular, are expected to be competent. We
feel we should be able to resolve problems, to take things in
our stride and go out and meet the world head on. Quite
often, the difficulties we face involve new learning and the
development of new coping skills. While demanding, this
can be a source of satisfaction. We can feel pleased to have
come through successfully and better equipped by the
experience to face future problems. Coping well can bring
a sense of mastery and personal competence which improves our self-esteem.

If the resolution of a particular problem is within our
capabilities, we certainly can legitimately feel bad about
ourselves if we fail to cope. However, some events and
demanding situations would be beyond the coping capac-
ities of many well-functioning individuals. One-off occur-
rences like major trauma or natural disasters are a good
example, but any series of crises which produces a build-

up of stress can overwhelm the person and create a sense of incompetence.

Our general expectations about coping and competence are based on normal life stresses and events. We all recognize that some situations are so severely stressful that the individual can be forgiven for behaving abnormally or being unable to cope. The stress created by active dependency tends to build up over time. The problem continues and there are few anxiety-free intervals. After years of crises and uncertainty concerned persons can feel like rag-dolls, limp and passive in the face of the latest disaster. The feeling is, "I can't cope any more," then in the next breath, "I'm a failure." To feel overwhelmed is understandable; to feel incompetent is unnecessary.

All active dependencies create stress but some put highly abnormal pressures on a family. Problems often occur simultaneously or in close succession. Some families have many problems: verbal or physical aggression, poverty, poor health, social isolation, routinization and lack of stimulation and emotional or behavioral difficulties in children. There also can be external threats, legal or job difficulties, rent or mortgage problems, unpaid bills and worrying school reports. For concerned persons in this situation, survival is the major issue. No reasonable person would expect supercompetence in these circumstances. Indeed, some would feel a strong impulse to help if they could.

Seeking help when overwhelmed is a coping strategy in itself.

It is not an indication of personal failure to request support when genuine difficulties create a high level of demand. In normal families, people rally round in a crisis. Because of isolation and fear many concerned persons are slow to approach others. By trying to cope alone they wear themselves out and don't get reassurance and support.

Even if extreme problems don't occur, concerned persons can add to their stress by making unfounded assumptions. They believe they ought to be able to cope when, in fact, nobody could in the circumstances. There is a profound sense of relief when you finally recognize that the problem is not of your making. The dependent person is out of control and needs help. Suddenly you feel, "I'm not to blame. I'm not responsible. It's an illness. He can be helped."

Of course, the stresses and crises continue while you work toward intervention but now you view them differently. Having become nonenabling, you no longer feel obliged to resolve dependency-related difficulties, though you may continue to be affected by them at some level. Now crises are opportunities to be used, rather than disasters to be averted. You'd still prefer a peaceful life but having learned about the illness and recovery you may feel you can bear with things a while longer in the hope of a favorable outcome.

Our definition of the situation affects both our stress levels and our choice of coping strategy. Where active dependency is present, the only real option is to work toward recovery. If you allow intervention to become your plan, you will have redefined your old situation in new terms. Now you have a goal, a new understanding of the problem, hope for the future. What went before was a nightmare, what comes next is hard work — but at least it is focused and purposeful.

Most concerned persons continue to be stressed until recovery has become established or a final decision is made about the relationship with the troubled individual but stress becomes manageable with support and the use of appropriate services. The intervention process is not stress-free but it does offer the possibility of normal living. It gives concerned persons a renewed belief in themselves and a sense of having handled a difficult situation as constructively as possible.

Establishing And Maintaining Satisfying Relationships

A sense of being alone and unsupported is not uncommon in someone who lives close to an alcohol, drug or gambling dependent person. As time passes, it is easy to become socially isolated. In some circumstances friendships are avoided from the outset because problems at home have always dominated. Where important relationships exist, they can be dropped or damaged as distress caused by the dependency increases. A desire to hide the problem, embarrassment associated with disruptive incidents, lack of funds for social activities or the general unpredictability of daily life may result in withdrawal from friends and acquaintances. Formerly enjoyable social occasions acquire a nightmarish character as drunken or unpleasant behavior by the dependent person becomes increasingly frequent. Finally these, too, are avoided. As a consequence, concerned persons may eventually lack relaxing and stimulating social outlets or become cut off from valued friends.

Because of loyalty to the troubled individual, a spouse may choose to hide the growing dependency from immediate relatives. Their motivation may include a desire to minimize the risk of an unsupportive or overprotective response by others. The problem also may be concealed to avoid worrying elderly or sick parents or causing anxiety to brothers or sisters who may have families and troubles of their own. Sometimes a spouse is blamed by in-laws and accused of creating or contributing to the alcohol, drug or gambling problem in some way. This is not only stressful in itself but its occurrence makes it impossible to view the dependent person's family as a resource.

Even where there is no blaming or negative reaction, concerned persons often experience increasing strain in important relationships. Protective covering-up or lying create guilt and tension. Conversation becomes increasingly stilted or superficial as taboo topics are avoided. The growing unease of all parties results in avoidance and the gradual deterioration of a valued relationship.

Constructive Support

We all need to feel supported, particularly when troubles are real and must be handled constructively. Concerned persons often need to develop a network of contacts to provide relief. Some rethinking may be necessary before this becomes possible.

We have a right to talk about ourselves and our feelings, particularly when we are hurt or troubled. By doing so we avoid bottling up our emotions. Furthermore, self-disclosure creates intimacy and is an important bonding element in close relationships. Quite often concerned persons hesitate to approach relatives and friends because they don't feel free to speak frankly. They also may fear criticism. Sometimes they suspect that others, out of protectiveness, will urge drastic action prematurely.

Self-disclosure does not necessarily involve spilling the beans indiscriminately. It is far more a matter of self-presentation. We can describe how we feel at the present moment without revealing the events that brought us to this point. There is a distinction to be made between facts and feelings. Where there are anxieties about self-disclosure in relation to dependency, facts may pose the greatest difficulty. You may not want to tell your elderly mother that you have been treated aggressively by the troubled individual, yet you badly need her support and concern. In presenting yourself, you can decide to outline the basic problem, the alcohol, drug or gambling abuse, and state that you'd prefer not to discuss details. You can then say that you would greatly value support and acceptance as you've been feeling alone and burdened. This type of self-disclosure, in which you describe your current emotional state and ask for the help you need from others, normally evokes a warm response.

Quite often, other people have suspected a problem and felt worried and uneasy. Sometimes they've known all along but were unable to broach the subject in the face of your reticence. Uncertainty creates a sense of exclusion. People who care are often more hurt by feeling left out than by learning of the true situation. It can be a relief for everyone to have things out in the open.

People living with an active dependency may need to recognize that there are limits to the support others can give.

When presented with a serious problem by a friend or relative, most people feel obliged to offer solutions. In particular, they worry when the complexity of the issue makes it difficult to resolve. This is particularly true when a concerned person expresses confusion and inadequacy. The message given here is, "Please rescue me" or "I can't cope." Out of friendship or affection, others feel forced to take charge. They will sometimes take steps or suggest courses of action which are unhelpful in the long run. Before deciding to disclose the dependency, a concerned person, particularly a spouse, needs to be clear what is being requested. Are others being asked to support or participate in an intervention effort?

Some friends and relatives are not in a position to offer more than emotional or practical support to an immediate family member of a dependent person. They have no direct influence with the troubled individual nor have they been personally affected by excessive drinking, drug-taking or gambling. Therefore, they have no reason to be central participants while intervention is occurring. Their role is a personal one, based on a valued relationship with the spouse or child of a dependent person. In that capacity, they can provide warmth, understanding and a listening ear as well as offering welcome time-out and support.

In approaching people in this position, a concerned person who has made a prior commitment to intervention can usefully give the following message, "This problem exists for me. I have learned an approach which may work. I would very much like your support as I need somewhere I can relax and talk things over. I know I won't feel right unless I deal with this myself so I'm not asking you to become responsible for taking care of me." When matters are handled in this way, both parties are clear where responsibility lies and understand what the relationship has to offer in this context.

Sometimes concerned persons badly want some personal input. The strain of coping catches up and people can, at times, become very conscious of the need to be minded for a while. There's nothing wrong in this. Temporary escape from stressful situations can be very valuable, particularly where it is seen as a means of restoring energy. If your family or friends offer this type of support, then take it gladly. It can become an important resource while you implement your intervention strategy.

On the other hand, there may be people who are influential in the life of the troubled individual or who have first-hand experience of drinking, drug-taking or gambling episodes. These people can usefully contribute to intervention. In this situation, a concerned person may choose to ask for help and participation. Clearly both parties will need to consider feasibility and decide how cooperation can best be achieved. The helper needs to be willing to become informed about dependency and happy to work closely with the immediate family in following an intervention plan.

There will be occasions when concerned persons' motives in disclosing the problem to others are not so straightforward. There may be feelings of anger and blame and a strong wish to have others confirm a negative view of the dependent person. Most families feel protective of their own. It is quite easy to present factual material which encourages relatives and friends to adopt a hostile approach to the troubled individual. This is not particularly constructive where intervention is the goal. Negative feelings, confirmed by others, can quickly harden into implacable, indifferent attitudes.

Similarly, some concerned persons disclose detailed descriptions of the troubled person's behavior in an attempt to elicit the sympathy of others. It can be appealing to present oneself as a victim or martyr since most people leading normal lives feel shocked and protective when they encounter distress. Their initial responses are warm and supportive and, for some time, the fund of goodwill and care remains available to the person making the disclosures. However, in most such interchanges, there is a tacit or stated assumption on the part of the listener that action is needed to end the distress.

A concerned person who continually seeks the sympathy of others for its own sake is rarely interested in a plan for change — despite protestations to the contrary. Appropriate, valuable suggestions are rejected and help-seeking behavior avoided. This is particularly true of any program of change which involves self-evaluation and the introduction of new patterns of behavior. The sympathy of others has become the valued reward. Gratification sought in this way bolsters concerned person's self-esteem but also encourages avoidance of constructive, problem-focused responses. Eventually, of course, people get tired. Sympathy evaporates as others gradually realize that change is unlikely. Some spouses or family members who behave in this way are eventually rejected or avoided by their former confidants. A potentially helpful and supportive relationship becomes soured or defunct because it is abused.

In reestablishing relationships it is important for concerned persons to be realistic in their expectations of other people and to maintain some level of awareness of personal motivation on entering new relationships.

While the support of others always benefits a spouse or family member working toward intervention, it should supplement self-direction and commitment to change.

Even where an extensive network of relationships is available to concerned persons, an intervention plan must still be chosen and implemented by the central interveners if recovery from dependency is to be initiated.

Concern is the keynote if the dependent person is to be encouraged to seek help. If family members or those close to the troubled individual need to express anger or rage to a friend, it should ideally provide relief rather than contribute to a hardening of attitudes. Acceptance of the illness of dependency is necessary for everyone involved with a problem drinker, drug-taker or gambler. When compulsion and disinhibition are understood, disruptive behavior can be seen as a symptom of the condition. Anger and disgust are lessened as a result. Family members or friends can be invaluable in allowing concerned persons to blow off steam. However, if intervention is the focus, it is important to use this as a temporary support which gives the strength to persist.

Sometimes strangers can offer very meaningful support, particularly when they can identify closely on the basis of shared experience. With people in a similar situation, concerned persons can feel free of constraint and completely understood and accepted. Quite often, close and valuable relationships develop. Isolation based on a sense of being different because of the family problem begins to disappear.

By joining Al-Anon, Nar-Anon or Gamanon or by participating in an outpatient or residential treatment program concerned persons can have access to relationships of this type. Self-help groups are a continuing resource for family members or friends of dependent people. This is true during both the active stages of the problem and the recovery period. Meeting others in a similar life situation creates identification, which reduces isolation. Feedback and support from others permit a gradual reduction in emotional distress. They also confirm self-worth. The 12 Steps and the program of personal recovery on which the self-support groups are based help concerned persons in a variety of ways.

The emphasis on dependency as an illness removes self-blame. It also encourages a reduction in responsibility for the dependent person's behavior. The recognition of enabling is assisted by the group process and educational literature. Furthermore, families are supported while pacing themselves in becoming nonenabling. The positive emphasis on self-care and self-development, within the context of personal recovery from the impact of dependency, is of enormous value. It is particularly useful for concerned persons who have been neglecting personal needs due to preoccupation with the behavior of the troubled individual.

In summary, establishing and maintaining supportive relationships is a vital part of constructive self-care. They help concerned persons formulate ideas and clarify feelings as they progressively move toward intervention. They also provide opportunities for relaxation and temporary forgetfulness which can renew energies.

Reintroducing Predictability To Daily Life

Most families need routine and order to ensure that essential daily tasks are completed efficiently. The unpredictable behavior of the problem drinker, drug-taker or gambler can interfere with the smooth running of a household and cause disruption and confusion. Missed meals, forgotten arrangements and late nights create constant difficulties. Families eventually become accustomed to uncertainty and disappointment. Stability is missing and people may become exhausted and resentful.

While intervention is occurring, the behavior of the dependent person will continue to be unpredictable and centered on alcohol or drug-use or gambling. However, family members and friends can do a great deal to minimize personal inconvenience. They can also avoid creating unnecessary anxiety and tension for themselves.

By becoming nonenabling, relatives and friends can learn to stop accommodating the dependent person's unreasonable demands for special consideration in respect of household timetables.

For example, most normal households have meals at an agreed time. They also have an established routine about the distribution of essential daily tasks between members. Disruption caused by absence or conflicting schedules is minimized by prior communication. An attitude of mutual consideration is expected and valued.

Where a dependency is active, these reasonable standards and limits may be ineffective in practice because the troubled individual is uncooperative. For this reason, family members and friends may find themselves doing extra work due to fear or the wish to placate. For example, some concerned persons feel obliged or pressurized to cook additional meals when the dependent person is late. This is an imposition and can generate anger and contribute to an atmosphere of hostility. Others feel anxious and unable to sleep until they are sure the dependent person has returned, even though they are exhausted and badly need to rest.

Any family member or friend in one of these situations will feel tense and inwardly seething. This personal response is completely understandable but, unfortunately, it benefits nobody. Because his unreasonable demands are catered to, the dependent person may become particularly egocentric and inconsiderate. While others fume, he disrupts. He eventually emerges as the household ogre of whom normal standards of behavior are no longer expected. Everybody in a family suffers when this happens because hatred and resentment develop. The dependent person also becomes increasingly isolated.

When concerned persons decide to set reasonable standards which suit themselves, they are being nonenabling. It is quite appropriate to expect consideration and reliability from the dependent person. Further failure to comply with household schedules or to behave thoughtfully can provide material for feedback and help create the conditions for intervention.

Sometimes, too, families or friends abandon plans for activities or trips because the dependent person is late or has created last-minute difficulties. This benefits no one. People feel disappointed, angry and cheated. Often time which could have been enjoyed is spent, instead, in an atmosphere of resentment.

Children, in particular, feel let-down and rejected by the nonappearance of a parent under these circumstances. Such feelings can be fed back later to the troubled individual to increase his understanding of the impact of his absence on family life.

It is more constructive for family and friends to go ahead with activities, despite the absence of the dependent person. In the first place, people are not deprived of an enjoyable event. In the second place, it underlines for the troubled individual that he is excluding himself by choosing to drink, take drugs or gamble.

Where it is possible to restore some degree of predictability to family life, day-to-day living becomes less stressful for concerned persons. Over time, a more cohesive family atmosphere develops with reduced tension, greater stability and improved rapport between members. Against this background it is much easier to work constructively, as a unit, to achieve intervention.

6

Implementing Intervention

At this point, we have examined the rationale and strategies of intervention in some detail. It may now be useful to consider some preliminary steps. These help create an intervention-oriented atmosphere and organize participants so that goals can be achieved. The following three factors are important:

1. Commitment.
2. Involvement.
3. Consensus.

Commitment

In our discussion so far, intervention has been presented in a positive light although the strains and difficulties have not been minimized. It seems clear that two initial tasks need to be accomplished by relatives and friends before it can become a reality. Those concerned must first achieve a personal readiness for change. They must then select intervention as the most appropriate course in their circumstances.

165

Developing personal readiness involves:

1. *Overcoming ambivalence and misgivings.*
2. *Reactivating concern for the troubled individual.*
3. *Accepting dependency as an illness from which recovery can occur with outside help.*
4. *Improving self-esteem and social support.*

Given this baseline, further change is inevitable since beliefs from the past and expectations for the future are revised in the light of new information. The central issue for concerned persons shifts from "How am I going to survive?" to "What can I do to make things better?" The first represents an immersion in the present with the future a dark tunnel, the second turns forward with hope. Internal disquiet with the status quo is often a positive, not negative force. We actively pursue change when disheartened by current circumstances or when we aspire to a more promising future. Relatives or friends who have decided to improve life for themselves and the dependent person are ready to choose intervention. Paradoxically the intervention decision arises from a lack of alternatives and the need to create alternatives.

A positive mindset is vital when pursuing intervention. It is essential to believe in the possibility of change and to hope that it can be achieved. An attitude of optimism is appropriate and useful. Firmly held belief is a force to be reckoned with. The possibility of improvement and recovery injects energy which revitalizes the family as a group. When gloom and hopelessness are dispelled, the way is open for a cooperative attempt to reach the dependent person.

A firmly-held conviction that the troubled individual needs and must agree to accept help sustains commitment. It also allows concerned persons to cope with temporary disappointments. Some interventions are very straightforward with results achieved easily and quickly. Others are complex or prolonged with considerable investment of energy and activity by relatives and friends. Where success is not immediately evident, disenchantment with the strategy can follow. Interveners, therefore, need to make a conscious decision to give priority to the dependent person's need for help before considering personal options to improve their quality of life. In any event, there are gains: Intervention usually works, though the time span can vary. If unsuccessful after sustained effort, the attempt allows others in good conscience to redirect energy to personal needs.

Involvement

Bonding is the key element which makes intervention effective. Interveners are central figures in the troubled individual's life. Emotional bonds arise through involvement and attachment, complementing daily association and shared long-term interests. Lives are interwoven in important relationships so that individual problems or progress affect others. When people are close, mutual influence occurs at a direct or indirect level. Influential relationships such as those between parents and children, siblings, extended family members, spouse or long-term partner or close friends form the fabric of the dependent person's life. They make a major contribution to his identity as a person. When satisfying, they also provide meaning, confirmation and a basis for self-worth.

What characteristics make relatives and friends such effective and appropriate interveners? In the first place, their investment of emotion, time and energy in the relationship gives them rights. They have the right to expect a personal return for their commitment and the right to influence the troubled individual. Most of all, their close association gives them the right to be concerned, particularly when they witness the self-destruction of dependency in process. Good acquaintances mind their own business when someone is in personal difficulty. Good friends make it their business to help. When the problem arises from alcohol, drug or gambling abuse, help, other than intervention, is enabling.

Intervention is appropriate for a further reason. Friends and relatives share another characteristic with the dependent person — a long-term investment in the future. Past association and previously valued emotional exchanges leave a residue, a sense of responsibility toward the deteriorating person. Recognizing that the troubled individual's continuing obsession with alcohol, drugs or gambling is damaging his personality and health, close friends recall better times. They grieve at the contrast between their memories and today's reality. Although hurt and disillusioned by disruptive behavior, the echo of old affection can remain in the form of goodwill. Friends who participate in successful intervention are rewarded by the knowledge that they are helping the troubled individual reshape his life and regain normality in recovery.

Spouse and family have lasting bonds with the dependent person. For this reason, they have a built-in investment in creating a future that is better than the past. These central relationships are, in their way, irrevocable — not in the sense that they can never be ended but rather that they can never be undone. Mutual involvement has shaped and influenced the quality and course of lives. The legacy of a bad relationship is an emotional scar which damages our ability to relate.

Working toward recovery is the beginning of healing. If intervention is successful, there is a viable future. To regain self-respect and peace of mind, family members need to give and to get. To help the dependent person is one task, to help oneself heal is another. Both tasks are initiated by the intervention process. The family, as a unit, is introduced to services designed to facilitate recovery for all. Furthermore, the process of intervention can prepare both dependent and concerned persons for treatment participation. The blanket denial of the troubled individual is penetrated, to some extent, by prior feedback and family members can quickly adapt to active involvement in group and family therapy. A positive orientation to treatment usually is displayed by people who have acted as interveners in a planned way.

Concerned persons are ideally positioned to intervene for a further reason — their direct experience of the troubled individual's disruptive and manipulative behavior. Their quality of life and personal security are adversely affected. Each day is cluttered with dependency-induced events and the negative emotions evoked. Anger, sadness, grief and hopelessness are intensely experienced. Peace of mind and tranquility become as elusive as happiness.

Who better to give feedback to the troubled individual? Relatives and friends have factual information and emotional confirmation of damage. They can present this to the dependent person in a mirroring-process. They can give facts because they were there. They can express feelings because they were affected. The material presented is irrefutable and authentic. When coupled with concern, it allows the dependent person to see and acknowledge that he cannot continue to destroy himself or others.

Another useful attribute for effective intervention is the ability to remember good times. Relatives and friends have an advantage over recent acquaintances of the dependent person. The latter base judgments on his current disorganized or manipulative self-presentation. Concerned persons know the assets and good qualities of the troubled individual at his best. Through feedback, they can reactivate his wish to achieve appropriate behavioral standards and reasonable expectations of self. While acknowledgment of personal deterioration is important in recovery, belief in a better self also contributes.

In summary, those closely involved or directly affected by dependency are powerful interveners. Their relationship gives them the right to care and to exert influence on the troubled individual. An actively dependent person intrudes on others by virtue of his disregard for conventional norms of behavior. Casual acquaintances breath a sigh of relief when he leaves but relatives and friends can't easily relegate or compartmentalize him. His behavior is intrusive but so also is his need — the need for someone sufficiently involved to help him get well.

Consensus

It helps to have consensus between participants while intervention is proceeding because full endorsement increases the likelihood of success. Informed and committed relatives and friends support and reinforce each other. Furthermore, the impact of their feedback and concern on the dependent person is maximized by repetition.

When intervention is planned, it is possible to participate, abstain or undermine. As a rule, the course selected is determined by the emotional state of the concerned person in question. Oddly enough, all three responses arise, in part, from attachment to the troubled individual. The decision to participate is based on concern and a desire for improvement. Abstention relates to a conflict of loyalties or fear of the consequences. Undermining occurs where an alliance reinforces the dependent person's illness.

In some families, full participation in intervention is easy to organize. Each member is willing to contribute to recovery by using the strategies which have worked for others. Consensus makes it possible to focus early discussion on planning the intervention attempt. Discord, arising from abstention or undermining, consumes energy at the planning stage. It may now be helpful to examine typical circumstances in which these positions are adopted by family members or friends.

Abstention

Abstention from intervention is not ucommon among teenage children whose stage of development creates a need for a close relationship with the dependent person. They are usually same-sex children for whom the troubled individual has become a model. During the phase of strong identification they display devotion and affection by unquestioning acceptance of his apparent needs and behavior. Quite often such children are drawn into this position by the dependent person's defensive attack on his partner. His blaming and undermining are believed by the child who consequently views the intervention attempt as a punitive rather than caring procedure.

Because of attachment and need, the teenager finds it unbearable to consider taking sides against the troubled individual. At the same time, although reluctant to become overtly involved, there often is a covert or hidden wish for recovery to occur.

Tactful handling helps keep options open in this situation. By understanding the child's fear of alienation from the dependent person, the other parent avoids forcing a choice. It may help to equate the attachment and concern on which abstention is based with the equally caring emotions underlying the participation of others. If there cannot be consensus about the strategy of intervention, there can usually be agreement about motives — "We all care but have chosen different ways to express it. Just as you feel you ought not to take part, so do I feel I should. Intervention has worked for others. We would like it to succeed for us. We understand your reluctance to participate but we ask you to accept our decision to proceed. Should you find yourself reconsidering at any time, we'll gladly include you."

Fear of the dependent person's anger may also result in a decision to abstain from intervention. This is particularly likely when aggressive behavior has caused upset in the past. This dilemma can usually be resolved by comparing the tyranny of continuing in the unchecked situation with the anxiety associated with the idea of intervention. Following reflection, concerned persons may elect to intervene on the grounds that the process is unlikely to create more difficulties than already exist. Of course, if successful, considerable improvement can be expected. In any event, intervention-oriented family members avoid creating occasions for conflict because they respond less to provocation within the household. As a consequence, the period of intervention may not be as stressful as imagined.

Anger (a classic offshoot of dependency) often is well-handled at assessment. Due to isolation and guilt many habitually aggressive dependent people respond positively to authoritative information about their problem. They can be helped to understand the impact of the illness on behavior and personality. On occasion new insight about misdirected anger occurs early in the recovery process. The tension associated with participation in intervention is soon eased for the concerned persons in question.

For other dependent people, recognition and resolution of anger takes longer. Both treatment programs and self-help groups consider it essential that this issue is dealt with in recovery. Prior to intervention, fearful family members and friends can feel comforted by this knowledge. The intense anger of the dependent person, though initially a deterrent to intervention plans, is likely to be modified with outside guidance as recovery progresses.

Undermining

Intervention is most often undermined when a relative or friend is enmeshed in enabling. As a consequence they automatically bolster the rationalizations and delusions of the troubled individual. Occasionally, such people are themselves dependent. For this reason, they are reluctant to review their own or another's excessive drinking, drug-taking or gambling. More usually, someone who undermines intervention has a deep-seated need to be central in the life of the troubled individual. This person gains gratification from feeling that a special understanding or relationship exists between them. The serious effort of other interveners can be neutralized by someone with these needs. Reassurance and security are provided unstintingly whenever the troubled individual feels anxious or challenged.

Although undermining can slow down intervention, it does not necessarily interfere with its effectiveness. Those genuinely concerned for the troubled individual are motivated, in part, by an understanding of the despair and futility of continuing dependency. They are also committed to offering a real alternative to the sufferer. Recovery gives freedom from compulsion, poor self-esteem, negative feedback and guilt. Interveners offer escape from the trap; underminers make the trap temporarily more bearable, although the sense of imprisonment returns. By continuing to offer help, concerned persons endorse the healthy rather than the destructive potential of the troubled individual. They want him well, those who undermine need him sick. Although the collusion of others and his own denial prevent him from recognizing his illness, the dependent person's despair and guilt continue to grow. Eventually he may prefer to attend to a message which says "You need help and can be better" rather than one which repetitively states "You're all right as you are."

While those who undermine are, at some level, antagonistic to those who intervene, it can be worthwhile attempting to engage or neutralize a person who adopts the former role. Undermining can be based on a lack of understanding of dependency as an illness. Well-presented explanations may be effective in creating an improved perception of the troubled individual's needs. Where this doesn't work, concerned persons face a more difficult task but it is still worth proceeding with intervention because of the options it offers.

As we have seen, it is not always possible to gain consensus about intervention among those who are significant in the dependent person's life. Success can, however, occur without full participation.

On occasion, it is appropriate to exclude a family member or friend from the intervention effort because they are finding it difficult to move beyond anger. A hostile attitude simply increases the defensiveness of the troubled individual. Those who can't act from a base of concern, may be best to abstain from active participation.

When planning intervention, it is initially helpful to assess the extent to which consensus is achievable. A full discussion of the problem, at an early stage, can be extremely beneficial in creating commitment. As dependency progresses, distress and embarrassment occur more frequently. Concerned persons often protect others from hurt by keeping certain incidents hidden. However, when people talk together about events and personal experiences, the extent of the problem becomes obvious. Misgivings disappear as speakers inform each other of facets of the behavior of the troubled individual previously known only to themselves. As mutual disclosure continues, a sense of urgency about the need for constructive action emerges. The prospect of intervention can then be considered.

At this point, the aim is to achieve consensus about the necessity for intervention among significant people in the dependent individual's life. When the idea of intervention is accepted in principle, relatives and friends consider the level of involvement with which they feel comfortable on an individual basis. In relation to this matter, it may be useful to think in terms of two categories.

Implementation With Endorsement

While wanting to help, some relatives or friends may be unable or unwilling to participate directly by utilizing intervention strategies. They can still make a considerable contribution within the limits of their circumstances,. They can help by verbally endorsing and openly supporting the efforts of others, particularly if they also undertake to become nonenabling during the intervention period. By adopting this stance, they reduce opportunities for manipulation by the dependent person. They also reinforce the message being presented by others.

Implementation With Endorsement And Participation

Those who participate directly are the central interveners. They have a close relationship or important role in the life of the troubled individual. They can convey concern, give feedback, use influence or leverage and repeatedly request that outside help is sought.

Sometimes, due to circumstances or lack of willingness to get involved, there are few potential interveners. On occasion, there is only one — perhaps a spouse with young children who is facing the problem alone. Is it worthwhile intervening in this limited situation?

From the dependent person's point of view the process of intervention exposes him to a new experience. Because of the changed behavior of concerned persons, he encounters a nonenabling pattern of response and a verbal reinterpretation of his problem and needs. Although approached with concern, he is also made aware that disruptive, irresponsible behavior will no longer be tolerated. It becomes obvious that he must seriouly consider accepting help if he wishes to retain his position in important relationships. The message sinks home by repetition and by the growing recognition that he can no longer rely on others to resolve dependency-induced problems.

These goals can be achieved more rapidly when a number of significant people make a concerted effort. It is quite possible to be effective with fewer interveners. The intervention message is about change and recovery. Once presented, it introduces the prospect of an alternative way of life which may become more desirable as panic and fear increase.

Planning Intervention

If intervention is selected, it is important that participants understand its purpose and methods in order to work well as a unit. As outlined so far, each intervention strategy plays a part in conveying the basic message in a form receivable by the troubled individual.

Aim

The aim of intervention is to induce the dependent person to agree to a professional assessment of his alcohol, drug or gambling problem and to accept the recommendations made. These may include residential treatment.

Interveners

These can be relatives or friends and possibly employers — people significant in the life of the troubled individual who have agreed either to endorse or participate directly in the intervention effort.

Basics

1. Those involved must accept the dependent person's need for outside help on the assumption that he cannot regain control alone due to the nature of the illness.
2. Anyone endorsing or participating in intervention needs to become nonenabling, i.e., no longer attempt-

ing to control or limit the dependent person's drinking, drug-taking or gambling or to protect him from consequences of excessive use.

3. An overall attitude of concern, rather than a blaming or negative stance is essential .

4. Insofar as possible, interveners attempt to avoid creating or participating in conflict with the dependent person.

5. Ideally those who intervene have access to emotional support and are committed to constructive self-care.

Strategies

1. Consistent feedback centering on facts, failures, feelings and fears, presented in a nonjudgmental way at a time when the dependent person is likely to be receptive. The aim is to correct distortion about events and their implications and to create a clear picture of the impact of excessive drinking, drug-taking or gambling.

2. Using external or spontaneous crisis as intervention points, the decision to become nonenabling is reiterated for the dependent person. It is linked with his need to seek help with the problem which gave rise to the crisis.

3. The use of limits and leverage to underline for the dependent person the serious implications of a failure to respond. Statements about limits or levers must be clearly presented and implemented as agreed when necessary.

4. The request that the dependent person agree to initiate recovery by accepting outside help is made reasonably and repeatedly.

5. Any cry for help is attended to and immediately translated into a commitment in the form of an appointment.

Overall Attitude

1. Constructive and supportive of the person behind the *illness*.

2. Persistent and committed: Short-term or temporary improvement is insufficient to terminate the intervention effort.

When intervention is selected and discussed further, it will become obvious that each participant has an angle. This is based on the nature and quality of his or her relationship with the troubled individual. Each will be aware of particularly meaningful feedback that can be given. Each will know areas in which the dependent person is most likely to be vulnerable and reachable. Those involved can also make a personal evaluation of the limits and leverage that can be used, if necessary. As discussion proceeds, a tentative plan emerges for each intervener based on escalating effort — "I'll try *a*, *b* and *c* and if unsuccessful, I'll do *x, y, z.*"

While the overall goals and techniques employed are standard, the content of each intervention is different because of variation in terms of individual and family issues. It is vital to remember the function of intervention, which is to help the troubled individual acknowledge and accept his need for help with an alcohol, drug or gambling problem. Although many important matters remain unresolved within families, the intervention period is not the time to open up these areas. The focus throughout is on the dependency and its implications. If intervention is successful and recovery begins, family and relationship difficulties can be dealt with in treatment, therapy or self-help groups.

During discussion about the intervention option, one or several influential family members or friends can help the group outline and clarify initial plans. Later these same individuals can organize and encourage the efforts of participants.

Informal "intervention coordinators" are valuable. They create cohesion and translate a desire to help into a firm commitment which dovetails with the effort of others. They also enhance the supportiveness of the group and may take responsibility for maintaining clear communication between parties as the intervention progresses. In addition, they have usually informed themselves about available services and are equipped to arrange an appointment when the dependent person is ready. And, sometimes, they're the ones who approach the troubled individual and simply *ask* him to accept help before the intervention proper has begun at all. Oddly enough, sometimes they succeed, perhaps because their attitude is positive but firm or possibly because the dependent person is secretly glad to be offered a constructive option.

Although of necessity we have talked at length about plans, strategies and organization, it is worth remembering that a simple, direct approach at the right time may be all that is needed to secure a commitment to seek help. When gearing up for intervention, don't ignore the obvious or miss a moment of accessibility because it doesn't fit the schedule. The sole purpose of intervention is to get the dependent person to an outside source of help which he feels obliged to take seriously. This can be achieved within one day or require several months of hard work. The intervention task is over when this goal has been achieved.

Do Not Revert To Old Patterns

Despite your best efforts to remain nonenabling and to implement intervention strategies, there will be occasions when you resort to old patterns of behavior due to frustration or weariness. Conflict with the dependent person may recur or you may renew your efforts to control his drinking, drug-taking or gambling. Because of fear or anxiety you may resume your protection of the troubled individual and thus continue to enable. While intervention is in process, your new responses create unease in the dependent person and throw him off balance. For this reason, any lapse on your part will be welcomed since it represents a return to familiar terrain as far as the troubled individual is concerned.

Discouraging as it is to revert to old patterns, it is vital to regard it as temporary and to resume your efforts as soon as possible. Perhaps you've heard the saying, "Don't turn a mistake into a tragedy." *Lapses happen, courage fails for a while but there is no reason to abandon the intervention attempt.* "I've had a bad day. I'll begin again tomorrow," is a useful statement to repeat to yourself in these circumstances.

While acknowledging the difficulty of implementing intervention plans consistently, it is particularly important to avoid enabling. Family members and friends who no longer control or protect the dependent person contribute greatly to successful intervention. When quantity consumed and frequency of use are no longer being monitored by others, it becomes difficult for the troubled individual to blame or use conflicts as a rationalization for excessive intake.

The absence of control from outside creates an inner awareness of the loss of control typical of dependency — "When no one is stopping me, I find I can't stop." Learning this is vital to the success of intervention. It allows the dependent person to become receptive to the notion of illness and the need for help. Similarly, when relatives and friends terminate protective practices, the troubled individual becomes aware of the necessity to accept responsibility for his own behavior. Deep-seated panic and fear begin to surface, as the realization gradually dawns, "No one will help me avoid facing my difficulties." When this message finally sinks home, the troubled individual is ripe to respond to an offer of help since he now realizes he cannot help himself. For these reasons, it is worthwhile remaining non-enabling throughout the intervention attempt. In some circumstances, an offer of help may only be accepted because no other avenue remains open.

So far our discussion about intervention has focused on strategies which concerned persons can use within a family context. Our primary emphasis has been on the gradual development of an intervention-oriented family atmosphere. The combined effort of members hopefully will prove productive in securing a commitment from the troubled individual to have his alcohol, drug or gambling problem professionally assessed.

A family may wish to conduct an intervention with the specific objective of getting the dependent person to agree to enter a treatment program. A one-off pre-planned intervention event can be effective in this situation, though an intervention of this type needs to be correctly conducted. It is advisable to seek professional guidance and to rehearse the content of the sessions during the preparatory phase. Treatment centers can sometimes offer intervention training programs. They may also have personnel available to monitor or facilitate the intervention event. We shall discuss preplanned intervention in our next section. However, where professional intervention counseling is not available, it remains important for concerned persons to plan for recovery. As we have seen, there are intervention-oriented steps that can be taken within a family context with a significant likelihood of success.

7

Format Of Intervention

Plan A: Creation Of An Intervention-Oriented Family Atmosphere

Aim: To encourage the dependent person to consent to an assessment at a reputable treatment center.

Characteristic: Escalating feedback, coupled with request for action.

Time Span: One to six months.

Basic Prerequisites:
1. Concerned persons have become nonenabling.
2. The illness concept is understood and accepted.
3. Concerned persons are committed to constructive self-care.
4. Anger/blaming/hostility have been worked through by concerned persons.
5. An attitude of concern for the dependent person prevails.

6. Family members/friends retain some influence with the dependent person due to the quality of the pre-existing relationship/strength of the current bond.
7. Concerned persons do not wish to introduce levers or sanctions of a type threatening to the maintenance of the family unit.
8. There is no danger of a physical aggression from the dependent person.
9. Concerned persons have worked through ambivalence about intervention and are optimistic and committed to the development of a plan.
10. Concerned persons have ongoing support to guide and reinforce the intervention effort.

Nonenabling Effects

The absence of behaviors aimed at *control* achieves change in three areas:

1. It increases the energy level of concerned persons by reducing their preoccupation with the extent of the troubled individual's drinking/drug-taking/gambling. Newly-available energy can be channeled into constructive self-care and improvement in the quality of family life. The resultant improved self-esteem and intermember rapport helps reinforce family members' efforts to achieve successful intervention.
2. The absence of control by concerned persons partially removes the basis for the troubled individual's defensive protection of the mood-altering drug experience. It also draws attention to the compulsive and rigid nature of the chemical use.
3. Absence of control allows the problem to become conspicuous and increases the likelihood of a physical or social crisis arising as a result of alcohol/drug/gambling abuse.

The absence of behaviors aimed at *protection* achieves change in three areas:

1. It forces the dependent person to acknowledge and face the consequential crises associated with ongoing alcohol/drug/gambling use.
2. It underlines the vacancies in roles and functions arising due to the dependent person's poor participation. In this respect, it both requests responsible participation and avoids creating a sense of exclusion and futility in the troubled individual. He is then forced to recognize the self-excluding nature of his behavior.
3. The absence of protection opens up resources and support systems for concerned persons who are no longer hiding the problem.

Consistent Feedback

Characteristics

1. Nonjudgmental delivery.
2. Appropriate timing, i.e., when dependent person is most likely to be receptive.
3. Given consistently, based on current alcohol/drug or gambling-related behavior.
4. Presented from a personalized point of view.
5. Delivered on a one-to-one basis by all affected appropriate concerned persons.

Content

Feedback of this type focuses on:

1. *Facts.* Facts about drinking/drug-taking/gambling behavior are presented, together with a description of their impact on the financial or social well-being of the family unit. Feedback of this type assumes amnesic episodes and self-delusion and aims to present the dependent person with an escalating picture of harmful behavior.
2. *Failures.* The dependent person's attention is drawn to any failure to behave responsibly or perform appro-

priately in a vital role with particular reference to its impact on others. It is made clear that the participation of the problem drinker/drug-taker/gambler is welcomed but only if performance is at an acceptable level.

3. *Feelings.* Concerned persons present the facts while describing and displaying their emotional response.

4. *Fears.* Concerned persons outline their fears for the troubled individual's well-being and the welfare of the family unit — if the situation continues unchanged. They underline differences between the predependency behavior of the problem drinker/drug-taker/ gambler (where appropriate) and current behavior. They also draw attention to negative personality changes within the context of pleasant recollections of the dependent person's former patterns of interaction and behavior. While stating their current concern for the troubled individual, they also refer to the likelihood of further erosion of the relationship should no positive change occur.

Positive Statement Of Concern

Nonjudgmental feedback is coupled with visible stated concern, so that the dependent person is placed in a tug of love situation. The desire to maintain the dependency is countered by the knowledge that ongoing alcohol/drug/ gambling abuse is causing anxiety and distress for others. This places the dependent person in a conflict situation. The inevitable anxiety and desperation, often associated with late stage dependency, are mirrored in the expressed concern of family members and friends. It is hoped that this concern will increase the likelihood of a *Cry for Help*. This can then be translated into a commitment to seek help.

Reasonable Repeated Request For Action

The request that the troubled individual seek help by agreeing to an assessment is presented in a positive light by concerned persons during each feedback. Outright refusal is likely but persistence and an attitude of hope provide the dependent person with an option which will clearly please family members and friends. This may also be secretly desirable from the point of view of the problem drinker/ drug-taker/gambler.

Refusal To Be Sidetracked

Under the pressure of consistent feedback which is likely to activate guilt and shame in the dependent person, temporary improvements in behavior or attempts to stop drinking, drug-taking or gambling are likely. Concerned persons may need to be firm and restate their desired goal — assessment or a professional opinion about the severity of the problem.

Start Not Stop

In discussion with the dependent person the emphasis is not on stopping drinking, drug-taking or gambling on a permanent basis. Rather, it encompasses statements about the damage occasioned by their use and a positive request for the initiation of a course of action likely to lead to improvements.

Summary

This type of intervention effort is based on a number of assumptions:

1. Nonenabling by concerned persons will escalate the problem for the dependent person.
2. Spontaneously occurring crises will offer further points of leverage.
3. In the face of concern, consistent feedback and a reasonable request for action by family members and friends the dependent person will find it increasingly difficult to rationalize and refuse to cooperate.
4. The restoration of emotional normality in the family arises from the resolution of anger and the adoption

of a policy of constructive self-care. These sustain concerned persons in their intervention effort, particularly if they maintain contact with a professional support system and/or self-help group.

5. The use of limits, the maintenance of normal family routine despite the disruption posed by the dependency, will result in a painful sense of self-exclusion by the dependent person. This is particularly true if they are accomplished in a nonjudgmental way.

6. There is a reasonable expectation of disimprovement in the dependent person, either in terms of health or from a social/behavioral point of view. This factor operates in favor of concerned persons.

7. Any concerned, nonjudgmental intervention effort is of value, in that it offers hope to both concerned and dependent persons. If unsuccessful, it prepares family members and friends emotionally for a possible later use of levers and sanctions should a structured intervention attempt based on coercion become necessary.

8. It is assumed that an assessment interview at a good treatment center will further the dependent person's motivation to take the problem seriously.

Plan B: Structured Intervention At A Point Of Spontaneously Occurring Crisis

Aim: To help appropriate concerned persons prepare and deliver feedback to the problem drinker, drug-taker or gambler during or immediately following a crisis arising directly from the troubled individual's behavior. The purpose is to create awareness within the focal person of the damage to self, relationships and the family unit arising as a result of the abuse of alcohol, drugs or gambling. It is also hoped he will be mobilized to consent to a professional assessment with a view to entering treatment.

Characteristics: Gathered feedback, with optional use of levers/sanctions to achieve commitment to an intervention plan.

Basic Prerequisites:

1. Concerned persons have become nonenabling.
2. The illness concept is understood and accepted.
3. Concerned persons are committed to constructive self-care.
4. Anger/blaming/hostility have been worked through by concerned persons.
5. An attitude of concern for the dependent person prevails.
6. Concerned persons have worked through ambivalence about intervention and are optimistic and committed to the use of preplanned strategies at the appropriate time.
7. Concerned persons have ongoing support to guide and reinforce the intervention effort.
8. The dependent person's defenses are rigid and impenetrable or he is absent or difficult to engage on a routine basis. There may or may not have been incidents of physical aggression.
9. Concerned persons lack the cohesiveness and self-control necessary for the implementation of Plan A but are thought likely to intervene effectively on a one-off basis.
10. Concerned persons have considered the use of levers/sanctions but are unwilling to use them unless a further addiction-related crisis occurs.
11. There are a *minimum* of three suitable concerned persons available to participate.

Crisis Point: This is any addiction-related event which concerned persons regard as problematic or threatening to the well-being of the dependent person or the family unit and which is sufficiently serious (in terms of its implications) to create anxiety in the focal person.

Characteristics Of Selected Concerned Persons:

1. Each individual has a personal relationship with the dependent person or is in a position of authority in relation to them.

2. Each concerned person has been personally affected by the troubled individual's abuse of alcohol, drugs or gambling.
3. Each participating individual has specific information about events of the dependency or related behavior.
4. Each concerned person is able and willing to become available for a structured intervention attempt should an appropriate crisis occur.

Nonenabling

The strategy for this is outlined in Plan A.

Pre-Intervention Preparation

Steps:

1. Selecting and engaging the interveners.
2. Preparing the emotional climate.
3. Discussion of levers/sanctions.
4. Preparing the data in writing.
5. Role playing/rehearsal of structured intervention.
6. Dealing with residual anxiety/newly aroused emotions.
7. Selection of order of presentation.
8. Selection of informal facilitator/professional intervention coordinator.
9. Planning the intervention event.

Pre-Rehearsed Gathered Feedback

The aim of this is to present reality to the dependent person in a concerned way, which minimizes threat and avoids activating defensiveness. Significant people in the troubled individual's life provide actual information about drinking, drug-taking or gambling events. The incidents described are preselected to illustrate abnormal or damaging behavior associated with abuse and to underline the extent to which the functioning of the dependent person in important roles and relationships has deteriorated. The emotional tone and comprehensive quality of the feedback aims to penetrate the troubled individual's denial, resulting in his taking constructive steps to deal with the problem.

The characteristics of this feedback are:

1. **Nonjudgmental delivery:** Concern is a prominent feature: The dependent person's defenses are not engaged if possible.
2. **Gathered:** Each participating concerned person presents a personalized account of their experience of the troubled individual's alcohol/drug or gambling-related behavior. Because of the variety of age ranges or relationships involved each person's presentation illuminates a specific facet of the dependent person's behavior. A comprehensive or panoramic picture emerges as the intervention progresses.
3. **Factual and specific data are presented:** These are directly linked with drinking, drug-taking or gambling-related activities. Generalizations and labeling are avoided and anger is not displayed.
4. While factual, the **data is affect-laden** and concerned persons are encouraged to be appropriately emotional.
5. A combination of weight of numbers, repetition of content and careful selection of the order of presentation by concerned persons are valuable. *The dependent person finds it increasingly difficult to maintain defensiveness and emotional impassivity as the intervention progresses.* The facilitator or informal intervention coordinator can play a major role in assessing the point of optimum vulnerability and presenting the available choices. It usually is preferable to wait until all material has been presented before requesting a commitment from the dependent person. In terms of the order of presentation, it is often useful to start (if possible) with an authority figure who has sufficient leverage to engage the dependent person simply by virtue of their presence and to finish with someone with whom emotional ties are strong.

Prearranged Appointment

This is very helpful where possible. Failing that, up-to-date information about waiting lists and detox/treatment vacancies should be available.

Anticipation And Resolution Of Potential Difficulties

Those involved in the intervention should be aware of potential difficulties which the dependent person might present to avoid following through on the intervention plan. These can be determined based on individualized discussion within the family unit.

What If Clause

Concerned persons must discuss and structure a "What If" clause and be fully committed to it. Discussion of levers/sanctions opens up the issue but decision-making in this area remains the exclusive domain of concerned persons. Tentative or impulsive plans for action are inappropriate for use in the intervention situation. Pre-intervention discussion allows family members and friends to explore options but resistance of any type should result in the abandonment of any problematic course of action.

What Are Levers/Sanctions?

The leverage option presupposes that concerned persons offer services or emotional bonds which continue to be valued by the troubled individual and which would be experienced as a loss if withdrawn.

Sanctioning refers to a course of action which concerned persons may select in order to underline the consequences of nonparticipation in a process of recovery. It implies a withdrawal of physical presence, emotional support or social recognition. In the case of an employer, it may include a possible decision to exclude the troubled individual from the workforce.

When used during an intervention attempt, it is important that levers/sanctions are presented firmly but nonpunitively. They are not intended to punish the troubled individual for noncooperation. Rather they represent a positive statement of limits by concerned persons based on prior decisions to engage in constructive self-care.

Levers or sanctions which are based on *coercion* are usually only utilized during intervention, if *concern* alone is insufficient to mobilize the dependent person to seek help.

Follow-Through

Should an intervention attempt which has utilized levers or sanctions fail, it is vital that concerned persons follow through and take the steps they outlined as consequences of noncooperation. This is based on the assumption that an intervention may succeed at any of the three following stages:

1. Feedback, coupled with concern, may reach the dependent person without the use of coercion.
2. Where concern and feedback have been unsuccessful, the crisis may be escalated by the introduction of coercion with successful results.
3. Where both concern and coercion have failed to achieve the dependent person's commitment to take a step toward recovery, the immediate and decisive implementation of sanctions may result in success. This may occur during the period following the intervention event, provided the dependent person is made aware that he or she has the option of reconsidering.

Role Of Facilitator Or Informal Intervention Coordinator

1. Engage the dependent person and neutralize hostility.
2. Maintain the prerehearsed format of the intervention. To keep goals in focus and to prevent destructiveness.
3. Support others.

4. Draw attention, where appropriate, to the emotional distress of concerned persons.
5. Present the intervention plan at the appropriate time and facilitate concerned persons should it become necessary to introduce the element of coercion.
6. Clarify decisions and commitments and summarize the outcome of the intervention event for all participants.
7. Ensure that the unresponsive dependent person understands that a channel remains open and specify who should be approached in the event of a post-intervention change of heart.

Plan C: Preplanned Structured Intervention Using Artificially Created Crisis

Aim: To help appropriate concerned persons construct a crisis situation by getting together to deliver feedback to the problem drinker, drug-taker or gambler. The purpose is to create awareness of the damage to self, relationships and the family unit arising as a result of the abuse of alcohol, drugs or gambling and to mobilize the focal person to consent to a professional assessment, with a view to entering treatment.

Characteristics: Gathered feedback, with optional use of levers/sanctions, to achieve commitment to an intervention plan.

Basic Prerequisites:
1. Concerned persons have become nonenabling.
2. The illness concept is understood and accepted.
3. Concerned persons are committed to constructive self-care.
4. Anger/blaming/hostility have been worked through by concerned persons.
5. An attitude of concern for the dependent person prevails.
6. Concerned persons have worked through ambivalence about intervention and are optimistic and committed to the use of preplanned strategies to create a crisis.

7. Concerned persons have ongoing support to guide and reinforce the intervention effort.
8. The dependent person's defenses are rigid and impenetrable or he is absent or difficult to engage on a routine basis. There may or may not have been incidents of physical aggression.
9. Concerned persons lack the cohesiveness or influence necessary for the implementation of Plan A but are thought likely to intervene effectively on a one-off basis.
10. Concerned persons sense an urgency about the need to intervene and are willing to consider the use of levers/sanctions, if necessary to escalate the intervention effort.
11. There are a minimum of three suitable concerned persons available to participate.

Characteristics Of Selected Concerned Persons: These are outlined in Plan B.

General Guidelines For Intervention

1. Concerned persons should be encouraged to avoid labeling the troubled individual as alcoholic, drug dependent or addicted to gambling. The terms "problem" or "excessive" drinking should be used rather than diagnostic labels. Professional diagnosis by an authoritative person is an important phase in initiating recovery.

   However, it is vital that no doubt remains that the problem is actually dependency rather than simple substance abuse prior to the commencement of intervention training.

2. The intervention process can be conceptualized as a graduated series, each step of which contributes in a progressive way to the dependent person's recognition of the severity of the problem. In preintervention training, concerned persons should be encouraged to consider the value of one step at a time and should clearly understand the workings of the defensive/delusional process in the troubled individual. They

should also accept the necessity for a gradual, emotionally-based assimilation of the identity of dependent person in recovery.

3. Any well-constructed intervention effort, based on concern, is of value in arresting the active dependency. The introduction of feeling-based factual feedback creates discomfort in the dependent person and also outlines positive steps toward recovery. Even if the intervention attempt fails, a new perception of self will have been generated in the problem person thus making it difficult to continue to avoid reality.

4. Family pathology and emotional dysfunction become obvious during the process of intervention training. Concerned persons can be helped by recognizing that the full expression of distress should be postponed until treatment commences. During intervention training, emotional and family difficulties are dealt with only to the extent that they present a block to full participation in the intervention effort.

5. During preintervention discussion, concerned persons become aware of facets of the dependency previously unknown to them during rehearsal of the feedback material. This process can intensify their commitment to an intervention plan since new perceptions confirm their belief that the dependency must be arrested because of its severity.

6. While the primary goal of intervention is to achieve entry into treatment, the troubled individual retains the right to choose to drink, take drugs or gamble. However, concerned persons also have the right to choose the quality of their lives. This may involve setting limits or implementing sanctions in a positive way.

7. Participation in an intervention process usually is intrinsically beneficial for concerned persons. It satisfies a need to act constructively and also frees people to engage in self-care. This may, of necessity, result in a decision to exclude an unresponsive dependent person without guilt or self-recrimination.

8

Intervention: Professionally Facilitated

The Heart Of The Matter

Margaret had been concerned about her husband Peter for some time — eight years, to be exact. His drinking had progressed steadily. It was affecting his work, his personality, the financial security of the family. Margaret had tried hard to persuade Peter to accept help. He insisted there was nothing wrong and refused point-blank to agree to an assessment. Stalemate. Margaret, however, was determined. She wasn't giving up. She arranged a session with an intervention counselor and was encouraged by what she learned. Despite Peter's attitude, there was something she could do. The children could help also but they'd need to prepare.

Having talked things over, Margaret and the counselor felt that the intervention should aim to get Peter to agree to enter a residential treatment program. They also discussed the "What if" option — what leverage Margaret could use to get Peter to consent if he didn't agree to enter treatment voluntarily.

The counselor met with the family and a close friend of
Peter's. There was Susan, 14, John, 10, Tony, Peter's friend,
Sybil, Peter's mother and, of course, Margaret. They spent
some time talking about intervention, discussing rationale
and techniques. The counselor focused particularly on emotion, working with each person to ensure that concern for
Peter was reactivated and could be conveyed effectively.

They met several times and were asked to write lists of
alcohol-related incidents which affected them personally.
The counselor was emphatic; they must be specific, de-
scriptive and appropriately emotional. They were to avoid
"You always" type statements and were to think of themselves providing Peter with a realistic picture of his behavior
when drinking. Their aim was to use the weight of numbers,
their key positions in Peter's life and their attitude of concern
to break through his defenses. If this could be achieved,
Peter might see how he was hurting others and how great
was his need for help.

As discussion continued, they considered the "What if"
option. The counselor emphasized that they must all agree
about this and follow through to the letter if necessary.

Margaret had already decided. She did not want to live
with Peter's drinking any more but she did want him well. If
necessary she would leave Peter if he wouldn't accept help.

Sybil was upset at this but, as Peter's mother, she was
equally committed to his recovery. She was a widow with
a large empty house. She invited Margaret and the children
to stay with her if Peter refused. No one saw this as a long-
term solution but everyone recognized that, despite his
drinking, Peter was devoted to his family and loved and
respected his mother. If they all worked together, surely he
would agree to accept help sooner or later. The loss of daily
contact with his family would be very hurtful to Peter and
would underline his isolation and loneliness while drinking.

Their next problem was location. Where could they all
get together and how could they get Peter to come along?
Tony solved this problem. He offered to invite Peter to his
office to discuss a business problem. He would tell Peter it
was to his financial advantage to come. This was a good

ploy as Peter was now chronically short of money. The counselor was also invited to facilitate the session and ensure that it was as productive as possible.

All that remained was to make an appointment for Peter's admission to a treatment facility. The date was set. The counselor reminded everyone to bring along their prepared lists of incidents. It was useful to have them as they helped structure the session and kept things focused. Everything was ready. . . .

Peter: Hello, Tony. Nice of you to come out to meet me. This must be quite a deal you have going. Very hush, hush. What is it anyway? Are you going to fill me in?

Tony: Thanks for coming, Peter. Come into my office. There are some people I'd like you to meet. . . .

Peter: Hey, what is this? My family? My mother? And who's this?

Tony: I'd like you to meet David. I invited him here. He's an intervention counselor. Margaret and your family have been seeing him. They needed some advice. They're worried about you. So am I.

David: I'm glad to meet you, Peter. I know you're surprised to find us here — it must be difficult meeting a stranger. Your family would like you to listen to some things they need to say to you. I think I can help make it easy for all of us. Won't you sit down?

Peter: I can't believe this! Margaret, how dare you do this? How could you discuss our lives with a stranger . . . a counselor? I certainly am *not* going to listen to anything. And, as for you, Tony, how dare you deceive me like this? Some friend! I'm leaving — right now.

Tony: It's understandable that you're angry, Peter. But I assure you everyone here is deeply concerned for you. Here in this room are all the people closest to you, who care for you. Right now, all we want you to do is listen. Just hear us out. It's very important to everyone.

Peter: What's so important anyway? What am I supposed to listen to? I suppose it's some more of Margaret's fussing about my drinking. I've told you, Margaret, there is not, repeat, not a problem.

David: We understand that's the way you see it just now, Peter. If you would agree to sit and listen to your family, I believe you'll understand why they're concerned. I think Margaret should start. Susan and John want to talk to you, too. I hope you can give them time. Won't you sit down, Peter?

Peter: Oh, well, it seems I'm stuck. I might as well hear you out. Otherwise, I suppose I'll be in the doghouse.

Margaret: Thank you, Peter, I'm glad. I want to start by saying I remember very happy times. We were in love; we did things together. We had such fun. You were wonderful to be with. I used to think we suited each other so well. We had a lot in common but we could disagree, too. It was nice . . . It makes me sad to remember those days. Things have changed so much since you started drinking. I'm not going to talk about everything that's happened in the last seven or eight years but I have picked out a few incidents which really upset me. I'd like to tell you about them, Peter. You were drinking and you behaved in a way which was completely unlike you.

I was particularly hurt by your behavior at my mother's funeral. She died suddenly, as you know, and I was very shocked. I was dazed. I just couldn't believe she was dead. I needed your support very badly but you seemed to be drinking or drunk all the time. I don't remember those few days very clearly but I vividly recall standing at the graveside when the burial words were being read. You were swaying and obviously drunk. At the end of the service, you started to hiccough. It was terrible. It seemed so disrespectful to my mother. People just glared at you. I don't think you noticed. I felt so ashamed but mostly hurt. I needed you to help me . . . My mother was dead and I wanted your support . . . But you needed to drink and I didn't matter. I felt so lonely and sad. Later, I'm not sure you noticed but my brother deliberately took you to a bar for a drink. You were glad to get away but it really wasn't for your benefit. No one wanted any further embarrassment. . . .

Peter: I'm sorry, Margaret . . . But everybody drinks at funerals. I suppose I got a bit carried away . . . you know I respected your mother. I was just drunk, I suppose . . . .

Margaret: Peter, my mother's funeral was a very public example of drunkenness but, in the privacy of our home, you've been incapable many times. Let me give you an example. One night at home, two years ago, you were completely drunk.

You'd clearly had a lot to drink before you got home and I suppose you had a bottle somewhere because I could hear the gurgle as you drank downstairs. You were swaying and staggering and your eyes were out of focus. I was still at the stage where I thought I had to get you to bed each night so the children wouldn't find you downstairs in the morning. I tried to help you up the stairs. You're a heavy man, Peter, and you were pretty much dead weight. You were half-walking but swaying all the time. I wasn't strong enough to manage and I knew you were going to fall, just before you did. You fell back on me and we both tumbled down. I felt stunned and shaky and knew I'd hurt my shoulder and hand. My stockings were torn and my legs were grazed. Your head was bleeding and I thought I'd better clean you. Although I couldn't use one arm, I dragged you so you were lying on your side. I'd read somewhere that if a person was bleeding, it was dangerous to leave him lying on his back. I was dizzy and felt like fainting. I was crying as I washed your face. You'd fallen asleep and were snoring. At that moment I hated you, but mostly I felt hopeless and beaten. I remember looking at your face, still covered with traces of blood and I recalled how you looked on our wedding day. I wanted nothing more than to go away somewhere, lie down and never get up . . . . It's so sad. It's the sadness and the waste I can't stand. This is not you, Peter . . . . I know that . . . . I remember how you were before you started to drink, but the children don't — all they see is someone who drinks all the time.

David: John, do you think you'd be able to help your dad see his drinking from your point of view? You're 10 now. Can you tell your father what you've noticed about his drinking?

John: Ever since I can remember, you've been drinking, Dad. Every day I hope perhaps you'll stop. I'd really love that. I have my list here and I'll read you the things I wrote that I particularly remember.

When I was seven, I asked you to come to school sports day. I was in a running competition and the coach thought I might win. I wanted you to see me. I asked you specially. I made you promise to come. Mom tried to persuade you, too. Well, you did come but you smelled of liquor and you kept saying "When is this race on? How much longer are we going to have to wait?" I felt really nervous and kept wishing the coach would hurry up. I was afraid you'd go away, without waiting for the race. Well the time for the race came and in the rush to get in line, I didn't say goodbye to you because you were talking to a man. Mom wished me luck but you didn't. I told Mom to be sure to tell you the race was starting so you could watch. I ran really hard, thinking it was the first time you'd ever seen me at a sports day and I won the race. I looked over to see you but only Mom was there. She told me you had seen the race but you had to go off on business with the man and you'd left me some money for winning the race. I didn't believe it! I dashed to the parking lot, hoping you'd still be there but the car was gone. You weren't there when I was getting the medal either and I didn't really believe you'd seen the race. The next day, you offered me money but I wouldn't take it. You just put it back in your pocket and said I was ungrateful, that I didn't realize how lucky I was and that if your father had given you money when you were young, you would have been delighted. After a while I was sorry I didn't take the money but you had gone out.

Last year, Dad, we went on vacation. You promised to take me fishing. I really wanted to go because we had been reading about it at school. I was really looking forward to it and had saved my pocket money for some special flies. I was sure I'd catch a fish. That was a terrible vacation. You took the car away every day by yourself and left Mom and Susan and me alone in the cabin. When you came home each night, you were drunk. I used to sit at the window and wait for you, trying to get you to promise to take me the next day.

One night you said you would. We'd go tomorrow. I was to be up and ready at eight o'clock. I was so excited, I could hardly sleep. I was ready but you still weren't up. I kept trying to wake you, to remind you but you were angry and told me to go away. I sat outside, crying. I decided we were going anyway so I got into the car and waited till you got up. It was hours. At last you came out. You were still angry but I told you you'd promised me and you said "All right then, come on." But we didn't go toward the river. We went instead to the town. You said you needed to see a man first and went into a bar. I waited and waited. I was crying.

At last, I got out and opened the door. I couldn't see you: There were all these legs and loud voices. A man noticed me. I told him I was looking for my dad. Then you turned around. You were mad at me but couldn't let the other men see. You bought me a Coke and told me to go out again to wait. You said you wouldn't be long. I was frightened but I begged you to take me fishing. All the other men were listening. One of them winked at my father and said he knew a place I could fish. He took me to a bridge over a creek and told me I'd catch a big fish there. I felt stupid trying to fish. The local kids were laughing at me. After a while I stopped. I got back in the car and cried.

Ages later you came out. You were laughing with the other men and they all asked if I'd caught something. I said nothing. Then more nods and winks. One of them went away. A few minutes later he came back with a goldfish in a bowl. They all laughed as he gave it to me. They were all drunk. You laughed, too, Dad. I'll never forget . . . We went back to the cabin then and I went to my room. The goldfish was dead the next day. Dad, why did you do that? Why did you break your promise? Why do you have to drink so much? Please, Dad, I want us to do things together . . . just like the other boys, with their dads. Can't you understand?

Susan: I feel the same way, Dad. I don't think you realize how much your behavior can hurt us. I remember one time when I had two of my girl friends up in my room. We were playing records. It was Saturday afternoon and I didn't think you'd be in. Usually you were out all day Saturday. Otherwise I wouldn't bring my friends home.

You'd been drinking and were in a bad mood. I could hear you downstairs, stumbling and cursing. I kept hoping my friends wouldn't hear so I turned up the volume on the stereo. I heard you coming upstairs. You were shouting at me to turn the stereo down. I didn't know what to do. I was terrified. My friends were, too. We just sat there, watching the door, frightened to move. You shoved the door open and yelled, "I told you, Susan! Turn that damned thing off!" I couldn't look at my friends.

Then you went into the bathroom but you didn't even shut the door. I felt so embarrassed. I could feel myself go red . . . I couldn't speak. I just had to turn on the stereo again, to drown out the sounds. It was awful. You started shouting again and burst into the room. Your trousers weren't closed properly and you looked grubby and untidy. Your eyes were red and I thought you were going to hit me. You saw my friends then.

They were sitting behind the door and you hadn't noticed them the first time. You didn't say anything else and just went out. We didn't know what to do. None of us looked at each other.

After a while, Jenny said she'd better be getting home. I felt awful. They both left. I pretended to be sick the next Monday. I didn't want to go to school and face them again. We avoided each other after that. They were never my friends again.

Then I was doing tests at school. I was nervous. I'd been worried about your drinking and so upset all the time that I wasn't able to study properly. I was afraid I'd fail. The morning of the first test it was raining really heavily. Mom asked you to get up and give me a ride to school, so I wouldn't get wet. You said you would but you'd been drunk the night before and you had a hangover. You fell asleep again. I went in to call you but you shouted at me to leave you alone. I was getting panicky. I'd waited for you and now I was too late to get the bus.

Mom tried to get a cab but they were busy at that hour and couldn't come for 15 minutes. I was frantic. I was sure I'd be late and I felt myself getting sick. Mom saw how upset I was. She told me to have a glass of juice and sit down. She went to ask one of our neighbors to drive me. The lady came and drove me down but I know Mom was embarrassed, with our own car outside the door. She had to pretend it was broken down. I was only barely in time for the first test. I was shaking when I sat down and I couldn't understand the questions or write anything for a half an hour. I felt awful.

I remember another time asking you if we could all join the Y and play tennis and go swimming together. You wouldn't even listen. You said you weren't going to waste money on club fees. But, Dad, I really wanted us to do things as a family. But you seemed to be drinking every Saturday and Sunday, so we never did anything together. I used to feel we weren't really a family . . . But now I don't care anymore — I just feel ashamed when you're drinking and I wouldn't want to go anywhere with you now, in case you'd drink.

Peter: Honey, you know I love you and John . . . . I've been so busy lately. Maybe I haven't been paying enough attention to you. I'll do better from now on, I promise.

Sybil: Peter, I feel so sad listening to Margaret and the children speak. I remember when you were getting married first — such high ideals! You really wanted it to be a success.

And you were so proud of the children when they were born. You loved them so much. The memory really stays in my mind. Susan was three and you and Margaret were hoping to have a second child. You both wanted that so much. We had a conversation one evening in my garden. It was shortly after your father died and I was adjusting to widowhood. You talked so gently then, trying to comfort me, saying the children were the next generation and had to be treasured. You meant what you said, Peter, and when John was born, you were overjoyed. You had so many plans — football, fishing trips . . . It's heart-breaking today to hear John talking of his terrible vacation.

Oh Peter, you wanted so much for your family before you started drinking. You need help. We want to help you. Please agree . . . I've been so worried.

Peter: Well . . . I suppose I hadn't realized I was hurting you all so much. Maybe I drink a little too much. Maybe I can cut back, get more involved with the family.

Tony: Peter, I know you love your family and don't want to hurt them. And I know you mean well when you talk of cutting back on your drinking. But . . . I don't believe you can. I've been with you quite often when you're drinking, Peter. You drink much faster than anyone else. Many times you've said you were going to the toilet but you were actually getting an extra drink at the bar. You gulp your drinks and people notice.

I remember one time there were four of us together. We were old friends and just having a chat. I was enjoying myself. So were the others. You came into the bar and tried to avoid us. Naturally, we asked you to join us. Reluctantly you said you would but insisted on buying a drink first. I distinctly heard you order doubles for yourself and you drank one while you were there before joining us — carrying another. You gulped your drink and were obviously more interested in rushing us to have another drink. You had no interest in the conversation but drank steadily.

You kept making excuses to leave us so you could have extra drinks. By the end of the evening, you were very drunk. We all felt uncomfortable with you. When we were getting up to go, you knocked against someone and didn't even apologize.

You insisted on driving home although you could hardly stand. You got really angry with me when I suggested you were not capable. I was worried about you and followed you home. Your driving was really dangerous! You went through red lights and went over the speed limit every chance you got. You turned one corner too fast and the door on your side of the car swung open. You didn't notice it for ages. In fact, I think it swung closed by itself.

Peter, you could have killed yourself or someone else that night. Before that, I knew you drank too much but that evening I realized you lose control. You can't stop when you're drinking. That's why I feel you won't be able to cut down, no matter how hard you try . . . You need help, Peter. I don't believe you can do it on your own.

Peter: I'm sure I can manage on my own. I've never really tried to stop. I agree to stop, okay? That's what this meeting is about anyway, isn't it?

David: Not quite, Peter. Your family and Tony, your friend, have given your situation a lot of thought. I understand you've made some promises before, mostly to Margaret. You weren't able to keep them. Some people lose control of their alcohol intake. It's a dependency, a recognized illness. Professional help is needed to help you to get well. Your family would like you to enter a residential treatment program. There you'll get the specialized help you need and your family will have an opportunity to deal with the distress they feel. I've watched and listened today as people were speaking. Margaret, Susan, John and your mother are deeply upset. They are sad and worried. I could see that and I believe you did, too, Peter. It would so relieve everyone to feel you were agreeing to accept the help you need. . . .

Peter: Look, I'm willing to stop drinking. In fact, I *promise* to stop drinking. But I'm not going into any program. I can handle it myself . . . Margaret, Susan, John, Mom — I promise I'll try.

Margaret: Well, Peter, I'm sorry to have to say this to you but I can't accept that you're able to stop on your own. We want you to go into treatment. We've talked it over between us. We're really concerned for you, Peter. We want you to give yourself the best possible chance to get well. We feel you need a program and we won't be happy with a compromise.

Peter . . . It's hard for me to say this to you but if you don't enter treatment *now*, Susan and John and I are moving in with Sybil. I need some time to decide about the long-term future of the family. I just don't want to continue living with you while you are drinking this way. I do love you but I want you well. If you agree to enter treatment now, we'll all stand by you and help and support you in any way we can. The choice is yours.

Peter: What am I hearing? Mother, you and Margaret are ganging up on me! This isn't fair. You're blackmailing me.

Sybil: Peter, we have rights, too. Margaret and the children need a breathing space. They're exhausted and very worried. Of course, they'd be upset moving out and staying with me. You can make that unnecessary by agreeing to enter the treatment program now. You need help and, sooner or later, you'll have to accept that. I believe you can't stop drinking alone. Right now, every one has got together in this difficult situation to try to get this across to you. Please reconsider, for your sake and ours.

We love you, Peter, and want you well. But we are not prepared to stand by and watch you destroy yourself . . .

Peter: You really are putting me under pressure. What's involved in this treatment program anyway?

David: I'll be glad to describe it to you, Peter. There's a particularly good program with a vacancy right now. Why don't we go over there and I'll explain how it works in the car . . . Sybil can take Margaret and the children . . . I think you'll be making a very good decision for yourself, if you decide to take that vacancy today.

Comment

As we see clearly from this illustration, Peter's initial motivation to utilize treatment is extremely tentative. The intervention process has given him a limited understanding of the impact of his alcohol abuse on those directly and consistently affected — his family. It is clear at this time that he does not consider himself *alcoholic*. He grudgingly admits that he is drinking a little too much or is less involved with the family than he should be. He displays no understanding or acceptance of the progressive nature of his condition. He cannot see the relationship between the unpleasant personality and behavioral changes described by his family and the toxic effects of chronic alcohol abuse. While affected to some extent by the material disclosed during intervention, his understanding of the distress experienced by his family remains limited. He can observe it when presented to him clearly, but he has lost the ability to empathize. Self-engrossed behavior, geared to ensure his survival as an active alcohol abuser, has become habitual. Prioritization of chemical use has resulted in his relegating family relationships and commitments to second place in his life. Peter's emotions are repressed, leading to lack of responsiveness to the pain of others. However, anger, as a self-protective response, is readily displayed when his drinking is threatened.

It is clear that Peter is agreeing to enter a program for assessment and treatment solely because of the losses involved if he does not. Any motivation present is induced by the behavior and choices of his concerned persons. To avoid losing his family he will enter a program. His initial attitude will be resentful and hostile. He will view treatment as a process to be endured, to placate his wife and children and to avoid worrying his mother. When introduced to fellow treatment participants, he will be surprised to learn that the majority felt obliged to begin treatment due to serious external consequences which could no longer be avoided. For Peter and others in treatment, it will take some time for negative attitudes to change and for awareness of reality to develop. Good treatment programs are designed to respond to limited initial motivation. On entering treatment, Peter's active dependency is interrupted and he is introduced to an environment geared to provide the input and support he needs to get well.

Intervention Conclusion

To date, we have acknowledged the goals, techniques and impact of intervention and reviewed some basic intervention strategies. We must now acknowledge the courage and generosity of spirit required for its implementation. While recognizing the tensions and difficulties that arise, let us also recall the rewards. Successful intervention is the beginning of recovery — a long-term process of growth and development in which both concerned and dependent persons participate as individuals. It is challenging but stimulating, demanding but supportive and the reward, at the end, is blissful normality.

9

Encounter With Reality

Peter's Reflections On Treatment

I'm here two days now — it feels like a lifetime. I can hardly wait to get out. Every time I think of Margaret and my mother pressuring me like that, I get so angry I could spit. Why didn't I stand up for myself better at that so-called intervention? I let them walk all over me. Talk about a sitting duck. Much as it sickens me, I suppose I'll have to stay . . . maybe it'll get them off my back. Anyway, they're exaggerating about the drinking. I was overdoing it a bit — but I'm still in control. I'm sure of one thing, though . . . I'm not an alcoholic — and I don't care what they told me in assessment . . . I know I have blackouts, can't always remember — but lots of drinkers do. I get the shakes occasionally in the morning . . . but, dammit, when I was at college, years ago, some of the fellows who drank a lot got them . . . at 22. Were they so-called alcoholics too?

Seems to me, in this place, anyone who drinks more than a couple of shots or beers is assumed to have a problem . . . bunch of stinking do-gooders. Anyway, real alcoholics are winos in alleys, not people like me. I met a fellow here in assessment. Now he was the genuine article. Shaking like a leaf; had to go to detox . . . Someone told me later his liver is shot to pieces, his wife left him his job is on the line. Some contrast! There's no way I'm like him. Hell, this place makes me tense. Here I am, thinking all these things . . . I'd just love to tell them exactly how I feel. But no, I'm going to be smart . . . play it cool, no hassle. The people here are mostly okay . . . pretty friendly, actually. But so what, I still hate it. I'll never forgive Margaret for doing this to me . . . I never thought she'd threaten to leave me. I still can't believe it. It's frightening . . . I'm so uptight . . . I've a pain in my gut and my head is pounding. I feel confused . . . I'm all churned up. I'm angry, afraid and lonely. I miss the kids . . . I even miss Margaret. I thought being here was supposed to help me. Big deal! I don't know how I'm going to get to sleep. Of course, they won't give you any pills either — no booze, no pills. All you get for free here is talk — and that is cheap!

A Few Days Later

I can't understand this group therapy. What are we supposed to do? Get all buddy, buddy and spill our guts? They asked me why I was here . . . how was I feeling? Some question. If they really knew, they'd run a mile. I told them about Margaret . . . about her attitude . . . her pressure . . . her nagging. Just wanted to set them straight before she comes in on Family Day. One of the guys identified with me — at least, that's what they call it here, when you play yes man. He felt exactly the same way as I did when he came in first and he couldn't understand then why his wife was worried. But, now of course, he sees the light. All is revealed! I should have called him Moses. Pity I didn't think of that. The tension in there . . . you feel so exposed . . . You have to talk . . . you can't just sit there and say nothing. And then they say things — see through you. One of them had the nerve to tell me I seemed angry. Who wouldn't be angry, having to sit through that? Still, they moved off me after a while . . . someone else was in the hot seat. One of the fellows was talking about his drinking — the things he did, how he felt. He really had a problem with booze and he still has a job, his family. Nice guy. He's near the end of treatment now . . . seems to be pretty committed to staying sober. Of course, he really needs to. It's different for me . . . I'm not as bad as he was. I must say, though, I was impressed by the speaker we had last night — fellow

who'd been through the program a few years ago. I liked him —
he seemed sincere. Hasn't had a drink since he left. Still, I suppose they pick the star pupils to speak . . . *pour encourager les
autres* and all that . . .

The counselors seem reasonable — shrewd bunch. They kind
of get to the heart of things pretty fast — talking about rationalizing,
minimizing, blaming . . . Still, they seem concerned. But, then,
they have it all set up their way, haven't they? Family Day tomorrow — Margaret will be coming in . . . I don't know about the kids.
Hell, I hate the thought of it. What's she going to say? Putting me
down in public. Well, I'll make sure I let her know what I think of
her treatment of me. And if she starts anything about our marriage,
I'll have a few things to say to her, too!

After Family Day

I'm exhausted! I can't even remember everything Margaret
said . . . things I'd forgotten . . . It made me cringe to listen. I had
no idea how I used to behave. Of course, I often forgot the next
day. I got a real shock when she told me about the night I called
her disgusting names and said I hated her. I'm not sure I believe
it. I couldn't have said that . . . with the children listening, too. I
know I'm mad with Margaret at the moment — but she's my wife.
I love her. Of course I love her. Can't feel much today — sort of
heavy, dead feeling inside . . . I'm completely confused . . . I
can't imagine that I did some of the things Margaret said — but
I don't think she was lying. She broke down several times, as
she was speaking. It seems she's been worrying about me for
years; frightened of the change she saw, concerned for my job
and my health . . . She was brokenhearted about John. She said
he's never seen me sober. Maybe that's true but I wasn't drunk
all the time either.

Still, she really seemed to care . . . she kept talking about
wanting me back, the way I was years ago. She said she's lonely.
Hell, if she really did care, why would she do this to me? It's
humiliating — it hurts. Still, maybe there was more of a problem
than I realized.

In the lectures I hear that it's not just the drinking that causes
problems — it's the personality and behavior change that goes with
it. It's like you become something you're not — aggressive, resentful, wanting to hurt. I'm not really like that — well, maybe a bit —

when I'm drinking . . . Maybe it was doing me harm — but I can't begin to imagine never taking a drink again. I'd miss it so much. I know they talk about One Day At A Time at the AA meeting . . . But, that's okay for real alcoholics . . . Maybe, now that I see the damage it can do, I'll be able to control it. Yeah, that's right. I hadn't thought of that. Being here will probably teach me to respect alcohol more — be more careful — more aware.

Group Therapy

This morning when I woke up, I was so tense and upset I was actually looking forward to our group therapy session. I really needed to talk. I felt I had to. I was so full of confused feelings. I felt a kind of bursting need to tell people . . . who might understand. Well, I did, and, I have to say, I was amazed at their reaction. I tried to tell them all the things I feel and what I think about Margaret and what she said . . . Some of the group identified with me — with the shock and disbelief I feel. They were very supportive . . . It was hard to believe. I didn't feel so alone . . . so shut out. A fellow who's almost finished treatment was especially helpful. He told me how pleased he was that I was beginning to talk in a real way about myself. It meant a lot to me, when he said it. I suppose it means I'm getting used to the system. Maybe I'm just conforming — I don't know . . . I just felt part of the group for the first time. I began to realize they might be able to help me.

One of the women was pretty helpful today . . . I was talking about Margaret . . . wondering if she could be lying about that night I called her names. This woman told me why she didn't think so. Of course, the rest of the group felt she was telling the truth too. If she was, then maybe I really do need help. Tom, one of the counselors, said that . . . asked me if I realized how drinking affected me. We talked about that a bit. Toward the end, he asked me how I was feeling now — as an alcoholic in treatment? That got my back up a bit. I felt I was being asked to commit myself to a life without booze, to a label. I hedged a bit, I'll admit . . . didn't want to be pinned down. I knew that no one was likely to believe I could control my drinking in the future. Let's face it; even at this stage, I've listened to enough lectures . . . they talk about progression . . . and you know what they say in AA, "Once an alcoholic, always an alcoholic." Still, I sidestepped the issue pretty nicely, I thought. Talked about the lectures and how interesting they are and how much I'm learning. At the end, Tom said he felt I hadn't been entirely honest with the group today but that, otherwise, I seemed to be doing okay. I felt relieved but oddly enough, a bit bad . . . guilty, you know?

It's amazing when you feel you have to stay somewhere — you can't leave . . . the group gets to be important. You want to fit in, you know . . . to be accepted, to belong. I feel better now — I know I'm still hiding . . . I don't think I'm fooling Tom. I'm not even sure I'm fooling myself.

A Few Days Later

We had a lecture today on the family's response to dependency . . . I was astounded. Almost word for word it applied to Margaret and the children . . . I can't believe families are affected so much . . . buried emotions; defensiveness; enabling. It was a revelation. You know, they call dependency the family illness. I never thought of it that way. I always assumed my drinking was my own business and not likely to affect anyone, except myself. Seems it doesn't work that way . . . Now I see it can't really . . . especially if you're living with your wife and children. They notice; they react; they worry. I mean, you wish they wouldn't . . . that they'd leave you alone — mind their own business. But you can't avoid hurting them. You hurt them by the things you say and do and by the things you fail to do — promises; commitments . . . I just squirm inside when I think of the number of times I was late getting home after promising to be on time. I often let Margaret down when she planned to go out.

Hell, I even remember a night I needed a drink and had to go out for it. Margaret was out and I was babysitting. The children were asleep . . . I left them alone. When I think of it now, I'm horrified. Anything could have happened. I was lucky . . . I got back before Margaret; the kids were still asleep. Margaret never knew about that — though we had a row that night because I was drunk when she came home. I'd finished off the bottle I'd brought back with me. Margaret never left me babysitting after that . . . it meant she had to stay in more. Oh, I feel so ashamed. What kind of father am I? No damned good! That's what kind. And I let Margaret take on so much responsibility, paying bills, managing money — even eventually earning her own . "Pin money," I used to call it, sarcastically. But I know now she often used it to pay bills. I didn't even notice and I certainly didn't care. How can she still have any feeling for me, after all that?

A Week Later

I'm sitting here, trying to begin writing my First Step. It's from AA and it says: "We admitted we were powerless over alcohol and our lives had become unmanageable." I'm supposed to use it as a guideline, to help me write about the ways drinking affected my life. Tom, my counselor, asked me to try hard to be honest — not to minimize or deny things . . . I've decided to try. I still don't really believe I'm alcoholic — that I need to stop drinking . . . but at least I feel I should keep an open mind. A group of us were talking last night. Some people had been in recovery a long time. They said it was a relief to accept your alcoholism because you lose the sense of deprivation that comes when you allow yourself to believe you could drink again. One of the fellows said acceptance was peaceful . . . I don't know — the more I hear in lectures and from my family, the more I realize how much damage I'll do to them if I keep drinking. At this stage, I really believe Margaret when she says she doesn't want to live with me if I drink again . . . I'd lose my family . . . and I doubt if my mother would be pleased. I feel trapped. I don't want to hurt them but I need to keep drinking.

I finally managed to talk to Tom about this yesterday. I thought he'd be angry but he wasn't. He said he understood how I felt but asked me to recognize the powerful grip alcohol has on me — on my thinking. I'm even prepared to consider losing my family — for the sake of a drink. Tom also told me that after what I've heard here, I wouldn't get any enjoyment or satisfaction out of drinking — I'd be drinking for oblivion: To blot out the guilt. Maybe he's right. I don't know . . . the thought of drinking makes me restless and tense — and the thought of never drinking again, makes me panic. I'm afraid . . . sick to my stomach . . . I hate myself, at the moment.

After Family Day

I can't seem to pull myself together. It's years since I've cried like this. I feel so guilty, so ashamed. I'd love to run away and hide. John and Susan were in with Margaret. The children told me all

sorts of things I'd forgotten. In the beginning, I kept apologizing —
but after a while, I just couldn't. It was as though I was using
cheap words, to wipe away what they've felt for years. Do you
know, Susan is ashamed of me? It seems there's some boy
who's been asking her out . . . but she won't go. She doesn't
want to bring him to the house, in case I'm drunk and, anyway,
she said she's not sure she trusts men. That she wouldn't want to
let herself be hurt — like Margaret. I feel sick. I must be the most
loathsome excuse for a man. I never realized . . . I had no
idea . . . They talk here about *delusion*. What a harmless sound-
ing word, for something so — malignant. And poor John. He
could hardly talk, he was so upset . . . He talked about his friend
Mark's father and how envious he feels because they do things
together. He kept saying he wanted it to be like that for us. He's
so hurt . . . so lonely . . . and he still loves me, still wants me. I'll
make it up to him, I promise. I have to; I can't hurt him any more.
He's only a child . . . I've got a chance with him — to get close.
I see now, these last years, the only thing I was close to was the
bottle. I was so shut off, self-protective — I didn't even notice how
John felt. And when I think of the time I humiliated him on that so-
called fishing trip — laughing when someone gave him the
goldfish. Cruel . . .

I can't think any more . . . my mind is fogged over. I think I'll go
and sit with someone for a while before I go to bed.

Some Days Later

I've just finished preparing my First Step. I worked really hard
at it. I think I was as honest as I could be. Since I came to
treatment, it's amazing how many incidents I've remembered.
Margaret and my family helped of course — their feedback gave
me a picture of myself. A few friends came in too — it was a bit
embarrassing but useful. I had no idea how much my drinking
was affecting them. They'd stopped inviting me places because
I drank so much . . . But then, I was so preoccupied with drinking,
I don't think I noticed. It didn't matter to me then. It does now.
They're good friends and I don't want to lose them. They care
about me and want to see me well. I'm lucky to have a chance
with Margaret and the children — if I can stay sober.

It's funny about that . . . the First Step really helped me there.
When I actually got it all together, wrote it down, I could see

clearly that I've been drinking problematically for years. I had all the symptoms: high tolerance; amnesic episodes; deteriorating functioning in work, family, social life . . . I could really connect my own experience with the lectures I've heard here — and with the things my group members talk about. We have a lot in common. We really help each other . . . it's great. You feel alive . . . you can respond . . . I feel good, at the moment.

I got some very good feedback from my group the other day. I was feeling lousy — full of guilt, remorse. They helped me see that this was positive — an indication that my emotions were *working* again: that my defenses were down and the *buried* feelings coming to the surface. Tom helped me look at it in terms of values. He asked me to assess which aspects of my drinking behavior made me feel most guilty and ashamed. I immediately said, "My family," although I was confused by his question. He kept on, getting me to break things down further, until we'd gone through my relationship with my mother, social life, work performance, social responsibility. I still couldn't see what he was getting at. I was confused. The more we talked about it, the worse I felt.

It was another group member who helped me understand. She said she'd listened very carefully as I decided the things I felt bad about. She told me it was clear to her that I had very obvious priorities and commitments — even though I felt I failed in my responsibilities because of my drinking. I listened but I was still unsure what she meant.

It was Tom who summed it up. "Peter, it's clear from what you say that if you could be the person you want to be, you'd be a family man first, a son second, a good employee third, a loyal friend fourth, a productive citizen fifth. In other words, these are the ways you'd invest your energies. These are the aspects of your life that are particularly important to you — some slightly more than others. What you've been talking about today, Peter, is your system of values. It's still there — still intact, despite your drinking."

I was amazed! I felt as though a load had been lifted from my shoulders. Without alcohol, I could be what I really wanted to be . . . I could live, as I believed I ought to live . . . I'd have self-respect again. I started to cry.

A few members of the group comforted me and one fellow I've become really close to told me he believed I was no longer able to see myself clearly — to see my positive qualities. He started to talk about them and so did the others — just little things they'd noticed about my attitude and helpfulness toward other people — my love for my family. It really made me feel good. I was all choked up! I felt they were my friends — they could really help me and I could help them. We could recover, helping each other . . . I felt so peaceful, happy, almost elated . . . and so grateful — to everyone.

Going Home

Tomorrow I'm going home. I was looking forward to it but now I'm scared. Will I be all right? Will I be able to keep sober? I couldn't bear to let everyone down again. I don't want to drink. I see now that I have to do it for myself — because I'm an alcoholic and I can't handle alcohol. To be the person I want to be, I'll have to be sober.

I told Tom how frightened I am. He said it was normal to feel this way — that he was glad I realized how serious I need to be about recovery. We talked about my aftercare program and my plan for involvement in AA. As we talked, he helped me realize that I have to take care of each day — make sure I do everything necessary to keep my thinking and emotions *straight*. When problems crop up, there's plenty of support . . . I felt better then. Other people have recovered. If I follow my recovery program, I can too . . . I know I want to.

10

Treatment

Treatment is a time of positive change and growth. A well-run program, designed specifically to treat dependency, is a resource for the troubled individual and his family. Treatment programs can be inpatient or outpatient, depending on the needs of the individual. An initial assessment by professional staff can establish the most appropriate service in each situation.

Few dependent people enter treatment with a clear view of the problem. Most are in denial. At this point, the troubled individual cannot see the implications of excessive drinking, drug-taking or gambling as clearly as family members, friends, employers or colleagues can. Defensiveness, self-delusion and initial resentment are common. The process of intervention usually generates a level of motivation in the troubled individual. However, the early days of treatment are a time of engagement as the extent of the problem begins to be apparent.

One of the major advantages of treatment is the opportunity it provides to examine the events and impact of de-

pendency in detail. Concerned persons are closely involved
in this process and have a unique contribution to make to
the recovery of the dependent person. Their involvement is
justified because their lives have been affected. They can
give feedback about incidents forgotten by the troubled
individual. By presenting the person in treatment with a
clear description of his chemically-induced behavior they
help correct the distortion that is typical of dependency.
Together with other experiences made possible by treatment, this newly acquired understanding allows the
troubled individual to accept the severity of his problem.
For most people this is a gradual process. The separate
elements of the structured treatment program are designed
to increase the likelihood of his growing recognition of the
need for recovery.

A period of treatment interrupts the active dependency.
It provides the troubled individual and his family with an
opportunity to understand and reconstruct the events of the
past. A good program will also facilitate resolution of emotionally painful issues for individuals and families. As relationships are reevaluated and satisfying patterns of
communication established, the family unit acquires an
emotionally healthy pattern of interaction. This can be
developed further in recovery.

There are several important goals and themes of treatment, which it may be useful to examine.

Goals

The primary goal for the dependent person is to sur-
render to the sense of powerlessness arising from excessive
alcohol, drug or gambling use. By accepting the unman-
ageability of his life, he becomes free of compulsion. As his
understanding of the disorder of dependency grows, the
sense of euphoria associated with abuse begins to dissipate.
Then the troubled individual becomes aware of his own
emotional pain and that of concerned persons. The personal cost of abuse becomes apparent. Eventually a point
of choice is reached at which recovery becomes the only

real option for the future. Then the focus can move to the establishment of positive self-esteem and the acquisition of the survival skills required to cope with abstinence. These, of course, include participation in the self-help groups vital to recovery such as Alcoholics Anonymous, Narcotics Anonymous or Gamblers Anonymous.

For concerned persons, the goals of treatment include personal recovery. Most programs provide family members and friends with a range of services. These are designed to correct the negative effect of involvement with active dependency. Acceptance of responsibility for individual growth is emphasized so that concerned persons can revitalize their self-esteem and establish a network of supports.

To understand the impact of treatment on both dependent and concerned persons, it can be useful to examine some themes which are present for both groups. These are:

1. Education.
2. Catharsis.
3. Validation.
4. Individuation.
5. Affiliation.
6. Mobilization.

Before examining these in greater detail, let us first outline the basic procedures and structures employed within programs.

Medical Evaluation And Detoxification

On entering a program, each dependent person is medically assessed by a doctor specializing in substance abuse. Active medical care may be required to restore health, though this is not always the case. To avoid withdrawal symptoms some people require supervised detox while becoming drug-free. When necessary for health, a period of detox serves a number of functions.

1. Medications employed allow for safe withdrawal from alcohol or drugs.

2. Medical and nursing care help build up the health of the troubled individual, to compensate for the physical effects of dependency.
3. The extent, if any, of residual physical damage can be established and a program of treatment initiated if necessary.

Basic Structures Of Treatment

Treatment programs are often organized around a number of core elements. Daily lectures, group therapy and counseling sessions are usual. Self-support groups (i.e., AA, NA, GA) regularly use treatment premises to conduct meetings. This arrangement offers considerable advantages to a person in treatment who is initiating recovery. An early introduction to the 12-Step program and the atmosphere of support provided by the fellowships is invaluable. Familiarization and personal contacts make it attractive to continue when the period of intensive treatment ends. The dependent person becomes involved with a lifeline which provides day-to-day guidance and encouragement in recovery.

Education

Education is a vital component in the recovery process of both dependent and concerned persons. Regular lectures, films or tapes during treatment help correct misapprehensions about dependency and establish the concept of illness. Topics usually include symptoms, progression, the denial system, emotional and physical effects. The aim is to provide accurate material against which individual and family experience can be measured and understood. Recognition and identification of common symptoms contribute to acceptance of illness and recovery. Other topics are of value in helping participants acknowledge the effects on family and emotional life. These include family dynamics, management of emotions, enabling, problem-solving and communication. A further function of educational input is the representation of strategies and skills which contribute to recovery. It is also usual to place considerable emphasis on the 12-Step program on which self-support groups are based.

Some treatment centers offer greater access to educational input than others, particularly in the structuring of services for concerned persons. Nevertheless, most participants in treatment are given the opportunity to reconstruct their ideas by exposure to an educational process. New learning also underlies the concept of self-help for the troubled individual and his family. This assumes active rather than passive participation in treatment and recovery.

The educational component in treatment is not limited to formal input. Professional staff have the skills to help dependent and concerned persons individualize their learning. During group therapy and counseling sessions basic elements of dependency are continually restated and related to the experiences of participants. By this process people are supported in the development of an attitude of acceptance. While painful, the dependency need not be disowned as an unproductive experience but can provide the basis for new growth and rapport within a family. This is particularly true if everyone involved can begin to understand that no one is to blame for the occurrence of dependency. It is an important event which makes an impact on a family, comparable to other serious life stresses. Working through its implications can increase cohesion, if the family utilizes the services offered during treatment.

Recovery from dependency does, however, involve a long-term element which those involved must acknowledge. There is no cure. People affected by the problem, including family members and friends, need to support themselves on an ongoing basis to maintain a good quality recovery. On a positive note, however, it is usually the case that most effort is required in the first few years after treatment, as the family unit and relationships restabilize. A further component of the educational element during treatment can assist in this process. Many lifeskills are acquired by all participants, including improved communication and social skills.

Important learning also occurs in relation to the expression of emotions and the processes by which painful issues and conflicts are resolved with the support of others. In these ways, the educational element in treatment participation can increase the life experience and coping skills of those involved.

Catharsis

Catharsis involves the expression of painful emotions in a way which relieves tension and accumulated stress. When guided by professional staff, catharsis can be an important element in the emotional recovery of both dependent and concerned persons during treatment. This is particularly true if new insights accompany the changes in feeling states and the person has a sense of working toward a goal — self-acceptance and an improved sense of well-being. It is possible to have misconceptions about catharsis, assuming it involves a powerful, prolonged expression of painful emotions. Very occasionally it does but the intensity of emotional expression is a highly individual matter. For some people a mild expression of anger or a limited crying episode can provide the internal relief that is required. The guiding element is the need of the individual. A treatment center can provide a safe, structured environment in which the expression of emotions is acceptable and supported as a part of the process of recovery.

People affected by dependency can experience painful emotions, frequently or intensely. Fear, anger, shame, sadness and guilt are upsetting and difficult to cope with. They affect behavior and can create a sense of being out of control. Inner tension and unrelieved distress can result in irritability, angry outbursts, hopelessness or depression. Of course, on a long-term basis, high levels of stress and unresolved emotions can lead to ill-health.

To avoid being overwhelmed by emotional pain, some people suppress feelings in order to survive on a day-to-day basis. When emotions are bottled up, tension is relieved on a temporary basis but the person may become detached and unresponsive. Sometimes people feel they don't care any more. This may be an accurate statement about the meaning of a relationship. It can also indicate a self-protective response in which emotions are buried to avoid pain. Treatment provides a valuable opportunity to express any backlog of distress of this type.

An atmosphere of support and identification with others make it possible for people affected by dependency to allow emotional pain to surface. As it becomes part of their awareness of themselves, they experience relief. Empathy and acceptance from others can diminish isolation and reactivate needs for warmth and closeness. Such needs are human, normal and valuable. They motivate us to make satisfying bonds with others and to give ourselves the right to feel good. As suppressed pain is reduced, emotional responsiveness is restored. Pleasurable emotions such as happiness, love and joy reemerge to balance and enrich the lives of the dependent person and his family. To survive well in recovery, it is essential to deal effectively with emotions and to be able to respond with appropriate feeling to changing life events.

When emotions are expressed with the support of others, an important learning experience occurs during treatment. Skills are acquired which have a long-term value. Both dependent and concerned persons learn to recognize the signals given at an interpersonal level. Nonverbal cues, such as the tone of voice, facial expression and body language, contribute as much to the expression of emotions as verbal statements. As people acquire sensitivity to the cues given by others, their perceptiveness increases. They learn to convey empathy and to offer comfort. By experiencing their own emotions and those of others participants in treatment also learn that emotional distress is usually self-limiting when effectively expressed in the presence of supportive people. We normally find it difficult to be in close contact with someone who is tearful or upset. We fear the floodgates will open and the person will cry indefinitely. For this reason, we give premature reassurance and concentrate on getting the person to stop being upset. We rarely intend to appear rejecting but a *hush hush* reaction can increase the isolation of the person who feels bad and leave emotional distress unresolved.

While participating in treatment, dependent people, family members and friends are offered opportunities for close identification with others. They also have the guidance of professionals skilled in the management of emotions. This structure gives safety and exposes people to caring models who demonstrate modes of eliciting and identifying emotions and supporting those in distress. By observation and personal experience unrealistic fears are dissipated. Over time participants become comfortable with the expression and resolution of emotional distress. This learning is of considerable value during recovery as it allows people to use the support of others effectively.

Validation

The typical dependent person enters treatment in a state of delusion. He has become unable to cope with reality and has erected a barrier of defenses to maintain his self-esteem. The *self* he presents initially is false — a product of suppressed emotion, rationalization, manipulation and preoccupation with chemicals. There is pain, unbearable self-loathing, fear and isolation. Normal emotional response has become impossible and joy and self-respect have disappeared completely. If asked how he feels at the start of treatment, he replies, "Bad/angry/resentful/anxious." Whichever term is emphasized, it is clear that he does not feel "good."

At this stage, if someone were to tell him that he has potential as a person, that he has good qualities, that he has an intact system of values, he would be astounded and skeptical. He would assume that he had conned the speaker into describing a side of himself that did not exist. For him the negative self that emerges during dependency is the only reality. He has lost sight of his resources, his aspirations and his system of beliefs. The positive side of his personality has been eclipsed by the compromises with himself and others made repeatedly during the active dependency.

Family members and friends are in a similar position. To a lesser extent, they too find it hard to define reality. Years of exposure to the dependent person's manipulation and defensiveness create a pervasive self-doubt. "Which of us is right? Am I or is he?" Reality, on a day-by-day basis, is shifting and fluid, defined and redefined to accommodate the deteriorating behavior and personality of the troubled individual and the changing self-image of the concerned person. "Who am I? What am I? How do I define myself when I live with a stranger?"

From the emotional point of view, too, many family members and friends have changed in an unhealthy direction. They use repression to keep the nightmare at bay. Some experiences of the past are too painful to be consciously acknowledged, but the anxiety and tension created by these walled-off feelings and memories are all too real on a day-to-day basis. Concerned persons don't feel good either.

So no one feels good at the start of a treatment program. Yet to get the best from recovery, it is important for participants to develop a realistic but positive self-image. How, then, does treatment contribute to a rediscovery of self? How does it help people reestablish appropriate interpersonal boundaries? How does it foster individuality while simultaneously revitalizing relationships? Together with other processes validation achieves these ends.

On entry into treatment, dependent and concerned persons are often in polarized positions in relation to their understanding of each other's needs, feelings and thought processes. The assumptions made by each party during active dependency create an inevitable tension. Each faction is viewed by the other with antagonism. The need to blame is strong. The desire to have someone take sides to support one's position is even stronger. Each group is looking for endorsement. How, then, can a relatively brief treatment process create cohesion? The attitude of treatment staff to each participant is the key — respect for people as individuals in their own right together with a willingness to explore all facets of the feelings and experiences which create conflict and distress. Much of the material families need to discuss is painful, some of it is heartbreaking. When staff display a supportive but straightforward response to the events and emotions described by participants, they offer

validation to the individuals involved. This includes validation of reality and validation of potential.

Validation Of Reality

Whatever the initial disagreements between dependent
and concerned persons in a family, it is important that a level
of consensus about the events and significance of the dependency is achieved eventually. Before this can begin, each
individual's subjective experience needs to be affirmed and
acknowledged as real for him or her. The reality of pain
needs to be recognized. Skilled staff can elicit distress,
making it safe to express the hurt and uncertainty of years.
Uniquely personal individual experience is validated but, at
the same time, tensions and misperceptions between family
members become apparent. Unjustified assumptions can be
examined when participants become ready to accept the
challenge of change. Skilled staff and fellow group members
can help the dependent person and family members to
become aware of misunderstandings, judgments and cate-
gorizations which sustain antagonism. The expressed position of participants needs to change — "My pain is greater
than yours, so you owe me" becomes "We've all suffered.
Let's work things out."

New insights can increase mutual understanding and re-
flective examination of assumptions from the past.

For example:

Staff member to wife: When your husband said he hated you, he
was protecting his dependency. Has he given you any indication
recently to suggest he feels otherwise?

Staff member to husband: Yes, your wife nagged. That was real
for you. And she is angry with you, you're right about that, too.
Can you begin to imagine how your behavior made this seem
necessary to her?

As treatment progresses, each side moves beyond polariza-
tion to a growing internalization of the experience of the

other. As the understanding of dependency grows, each participant becomes more able to empathize with the other's position. Concerned persons grasp ideas — compulsion, powerlessness, disinhibition — and begin to rethink. The troubled individual becomes aware of emotional distress within the family and of the deviation from normal behavioral standards which occurred while he was drinking, drug-taking or gambling. The reality of the impact of dependency on all those involved is now clearly seen. There is also a growing consensus about its appropriate interpretation. The concept of illness becomes accepted and its emotional, social and physical implications understood. When joint experiences can be interpreted in this context, treatment participants become free to explore current feelings and to evaluate the potential for growth within important relationships.

Validation Of Potential

At the time of treatment few dependent people or those affected by it are aware of their full potential or in a position to realize it. In the case of the troubled individual, the "negative self" has eclipsed the more positive, healthy personality. This is also true for some concerned persons but, for the most part, family members feel suppressed as individuals by the impact of dependency. For these reasons, all treatment participants need an experience by which personal potential is endorsed. This usually occurs in two ways. Objective worth, as perceived by others, is an important element while the potential for growth and change of each individual is another.

Staff members and people involved in the treatment process can often see the positive qualities of a spouse, dependent person or other concerned person. Apart from personal assets, respect is also given for their strength in surviving the many difficulties and traumas of dependency. A typical statement from others might be, "We understand it was very difficult for you to deal with such a painful experience. But you got through it then and you're talking about it now. You're doing fine." By implication, the message is conveyed, "You can change the way you feel and the way you handle difficulties." This emphasis on growth, choice and self-direction underpins the entire process of treatment. Each person is perceived as potent, having the right and the ability to modify patterns of response and behavior which do not work effectively. The aim is to help people meet needs in the present and future while respecting the right of others to do the same. In this way, valid boundaries become established and old myths about relationships are dispelled. The communication myth, "You should be able to read my mind," is challenged. The "How can I be happy if you're not" idea is dispelled. The "I need you to survive" assumption is abandoned. Participants move toward personal responsibility, responsibility for creating the interpersonal environment in which they can thrive, for asking clearly for what they need from others and for recognizing their individuality as persons and their coping resources.

As treatment progresses, changes in the functioning of individual participants become obvious. New patterns of behavior are established and improved self-worth and self-direction create further improvements in interpersonal relationships. The experience is positive; a resurgence of hope occurs. Although guided while undergoing this change process, ideally both dependent people and family members leave the intensive phase of treatment owning the new self. "The effort was mine; the rewards are mine. I feel good about the way I've handled things." This is a very positive note on which to begin a future in recovery.

Individuation

We all like to be treated as the unique individuals we are. Good treatment programs and self-help groups adopt a personalized approach to participants as a matter of course since respect for individuality is an important value.

In discussing individuation during treatment, however, we must also include another component — the individualized therapeutic response to the needs of each family unit and each concerned and dependent person. Treatment per-

sonnel are aware of the varying starting-points of participants in a program. For example, some dependent people
enter treatment in total denial, while others display a level
of acknowledgment of the problem. Some will have func-
tioned effectively prior to the onset of excessive drinking,
drug-taking or gambling and others will never have experienced a balanced phase of life. Family background and
life history will also vary between participants, with some
exposed to trauma and rejection and others to warmth and
affection. Concerned persons also bring varying life experiences and self-concepts to the treatment setting. People's
needs, strengths and resources vary considerably and this
factor can affect the pace at which change occurs.

The overall aim of treatment is clear — initiation and
support of a recovery, which will, hopefully, be long-term.
However, individual uniqueness in relation to life experience,
current functioning and personal goals necessitates an indi-
viduated approach to the provision of service. Most treatment programs have a standard structure or core of
therapeutic activities in which everyone participates. Specialist additional services usually are offered whenever they
are likely to be beneficial to the users.

With both concerned and dependent persons three basic
issues must be considered in relation to individuals. These
are:

1. The starting point.
2. Goals to be achieved.
3. The pace of change.

If, at the start of treatment, a spouse is very depleted, this
needs to be acknowledged in terms of work to be done.
Considerable support and endorsement will be required
initially before improvements in self-esteem and self-direction can be anticipated. Such a spouse may also have difficulty adapting to new demands and may become over-
stressed by minor requirements involving any change in
behavior or thinking patterns. A spouse whose emotions are
repressed may experience other difficulties. It can be
initially upsetting to enter a treatment environment which

permits the expression of emotions. Such a spouse is stimulated, but also threatened, by the intensity of feeling of others and will need empathy and reassurance before it feels safe enough to allow buried emotional pain to emerge. The same principle applies in relation to dependent people. Some display greater resistance to feedback and are slower to discard defenses than others.

Concerned and dependent people also vary in relation to early experience of family life. A heavy-drinking or drug-taking parent may have contributed to unhappiness or confusion during childhood, leaving a residue of personal distress in the adult. With the use of specialist services such issues can be reviewed and resolved during treatment and aftercare, freeing the person emotionally from the constraints imposed by painful past experience.

When treatment programs are well-designed, the individual needs and starting-point of each participant can be identified. Therapeutic input can then be geared toward helping each person make progress at a manageable pace.

During the course of treatment the individual needs of participants, in their role as partners and family members, also become apparent. Some couples and families clearly require additional marital or family therapy in order to make a good adjustment in recovery. Good programs try to meet these individualized needs. Their overall commitment is to the facilitation of recovery and the healthy emotional development of treatment participants and their families.

Affiliation

To offset the isolating effect of dependency, it is necessary to establish warm, healthy relationships. These are invaluable during the treatment process and also serve as an ongoing resource in recovery. One effect of treatment is to bring together individuals and families who share an important basis for identification — their common experience of dependency. A confidential, professionally-run program provides a safe setting in which painful events can be described openly. Ease of communication is possible because of mutual understanding and empathy. People are also drawn together by their need for support during the process of change which accompanies recovery. Affiliation, then, is facilitated by the group-based structure of services during treatment. It involves the formation of new relationships and the reaffirmation of existing bonds. New or revitalized interpersonal attachments offer dependent and concerned persons a healthy alternative to isolation and pain. As relationships are established, treatment participants begin to avail of the resources provided by people — emotional support, honest feedback and identification. In the long term, recovery is enhanced by a healthy substitution of support-seeking behavior when difficulties or anxieties arise. This is true both of people undergoing treatment and of family members and friends. It may now be helpful to take a closer look at some of the issues which influence the effectiveness of affiliation.

Trust

The expertise provided by professional staff contributes to the establishment of trust during the initial stage of engagement in treatment. The experience of participating in a treatment process, whether as a dependent or concerned person, ideally becomes an important period of input and review. Commitment is required if vital changes in self-concept, family structure, understanding of dependency and emotional functioning are to occur in a constructive way. At some point, both family members and the person in treatment need to experience an element of trust — "I'm in the right place. They understand me here." When trust is established, barriers to emotional expression are lowered.

The emphasis on self-disclosure with support which underpins treatment makes it possible for exploration of the impact of dependency to begin. As events are described and emotional distress revealed the classic responses to dependency become obvious. Identification between participants furthers their recognition that the concept of *illness* makes sense of the experiences people share during its

active phase. A new perception of self begins to develop as
dependent and concerned persons recognize the price tag
which accompanies enmeshment in dependency. Personal
deterioration, negative thinking and overwhelming painful
emotions begin to be seen as residues of the illness which
need to be eliminated if healing is to occur.

Accepting Responsibility

Accepting responsibility for personal recovery is an important task of the later phase of treatment. "I've changed
over the years. I'd like to feel good again. If I want things to
improve I'll have to work on myself." Support, warmth and
the empathy of others are important elements in the initial
healing of emotional pain and diminished self-esteem. As
barriers to self-disclosure are examined and discarded, a
sense of ease and acceptance replaces fear and isolation. In
this context, a new positive self can emerge which is self-
affirming and committed to personal growth. This vital
change is facilitated by involvement with others since reciprocal giving and receiving rebuilds self-esteem and confidence. A new pattern and depth of communication
emerges, as participants feel safe to explore their own
experiences and those of others, without risk of rejection.
At some point both dependent and concerned persons
begin to understand the extent to which everyone involved
is seriously affected by active dependency because of the
nature and progress of the illness. It begins to seem obvious
that no one is to blame. The condition cannot be reversed
once established and uninterrupted. Its destructiveness lac-
erates the family unit. With developing empathy and understanding of the suffering experienced by everyone,
forgiveness and emotional reconciliation can begin within
families. It then becomes possible for participants to work
toward freeing themselves of the painful emotional residues
of the past and becoming oriented to their needs in recovery. Ideally speaking, the dependency becomes *our* problem. Individualized interpretation of the meaning of a
family's experience during the active phase of the illness is

challenged. The dependent person can now be viewed as a victim of a condition which affects people across the board in all social groups. Spouse, children, relatives and friends can move beyond self-blame, disappointment and emotional pain. They can begin to understand their typical response to the demands of dependency and recognize the limitations this imposes on personal development and family stability. With the guidance of staff and the support of fellow treatment participants those affected by dependency become open to change. During this phase of treatment new and effective patterns of behavior begin to emerge. Relationships also are explored in order to reestablish meaning and define a framework in which further development can occur during recovery.

At the end of treatment, both dependent and concerned persons should, ideally, have begun to assume responsibility for personal recovery. This is indicated by participants' openness to self-evaluation and a new acknowledgment of the individuality and needs of others. At this time the element of affiliation offers supportive relationships. These become a channel through which positive feedback can be given about personal qualities and resources of participants, as viewed by others. This contributes to an emerging sense of self-direction and improved self-esteem of the participants in treatment. By now, both dependent and concerned persons begin to be ready for the challenges of recovery when treatment ends. They now have a network of supportive relationships in which they can feel understood and accepted but which help them maintain the momentum of change. While the prospect of recovery and normality is hopeful, it is also essential that people recognize the necessity for a serious attitude to self-support and growth. Success can be achieved, provided participants commit themselves to using the structures and relationships which were established during treatment.

Mobilization

By the time people affected by dependency are ready to use a treatment program they have usually experienced failure in the past. Previous efforts to resolve the problem within the family have not worked. It is very important then that treatment participation inspires hope — hope of a favorable outcome, hope of a better future. It also is necessary for participants to feel potent again; to feel that they can, in some real way, regain control of the direction of their lives. Both dependent and concerned persons need to become actively involved in creating the conditions for recovery. Treatment participation, therefore, implies an element of mobilization, which helps achieve these aims.

By emphasizing honest self-disclosure and by making group-based professionally facilitated services available to all participants, treatment programs create new norms or rules for social interaction. Honesty, openness, respect for others, mutual involvement, responsibility for self, responsibility toward others and supportive attitudes are emphasized. In this environment, it becomes possible for people to communicate in a new and effective way. Permission is given for discussion of subjects and the expression of feelings which are normally avoided during social exchanges. Positive and negative sides of self can be expressed. As people become known to others and identify with each other's difficulties, a sense of involvement replaces isolation. Concealment of worries, anxieties and problematic patterns of behavior become increasingly unnecessary in this atmosphere of acceptance.

Though initially threatened by the level of honesty, participants begin to experience the sheer relief of unrestricted self-expression. The emotional burden of loneliness and distress gradually dissipates. A healthy attitude to relationships develops as participants acquire a belief in the validity of their responses and a greater confidence in their right to be heard. Self-esteem improves and people feel stimulated and energized by the response they receive. Both dependent and concerned persons become increasingly aware of their impact on others. As treatment progresses, feedback is more likely to be positive than negative as identification, empathy and mutual concern create firm bonds.

A genuine recognition of other people as a resource begins to emerge. By the end of treatment, participants have acquired essential interpersonal skills including self-expression and responsiveness toward others. They therefore become mobilized to take the steps necessary to meet emotional and social needs while in recovery.

As treatment participants become committed to personal growth, they receive further help from recovering dependent and concerned persons who contribute to the educational component in treatment or work as counselors within the service. Their good quality, well-established recovery allows them to operate as models for current participants. Their presence in the treatment system is inspirational — demonstrating the reality of recovery in a tangible way. Their adjustment to a new life also underlines its availability for anyone willing to do the necessary personal work and follow the guidelines for recovery.

The mobilization element in treatment also contributes to the deepening of motivation for recovery. The initial motivation of a dependent person in treatment is often induced by external factors: family or work-based intervention, financial or legal problems. Consent in the form of "I have to" must eventually become "I want to" as the troubled individual's motivation develops. Several important elements in treatment contribute — feedback from concerned persons educational input, identification with others, modeling of self on those in recovery and the emergence of positive personal qualities and attibutes. Developing recognition of the emotional pain, loss of dignity, distress and disregard for others help the dependent person accept fully that drinking, drug-taking or gambling were destructive. With understanding a new life in recovery is chosen. With the guidance of staff, plans can be made to deal effectively with difficulties that may arise as the family reestablishes itself.

Summary Of Treatment

Full, active participation in a treatment program is both demanding and rewarding. It requires an emphasis on personal growth in both dependent and concerned persons. It is a time of review and revitalization. The pain of dependency can be explored and its accompanying distress resolved in a therapeutic way. For those willing to involve themselves wholeheartedly there is improved self-esteem and the development of valued new relationships.

Some families accomplish a great deal during the phase of intensive treatment. Relationships are reestablished and commitments renewed. Skills are acquired which improve communication. Both dependent and concerned persons learn to function in an emotionally healthy way and to work closely with others to acquire perspective and get the support needed to deal with difficulties. Other families achieve less. Ambivalence about the future of the spousal relationship is sometimes not fully resolved during treatment. At the end of the intensive program some partners are aware that the relationship is on trial. Others choose to separate or to maintain a preexisting state of separation. These decisions are often appropriate since realistically, not all participants enter a treatment program certain of their long-term commitment to maintain the family as a unit.

Intensive treatment, then, is not designed to achieve automatic reconciliation between estranged partners. What it does, however, is provide a secure venue in which the nuances of feeling within relationships can be explored with professional guidance. Choices and decisions are made by the individuals directly involved. Whether a new beginning, an agreed ending or a wait-and-see policy is selected most programs continue to offer service when the intensive treatment period ends. *Aftercare* is the name usually given to the services provided during the period of early recovery. Most such programs offer facilities to both dependent and concerned persons.

Aftercare programs usually have several broad aims:

1. To consolidate the recovery of the dependent person by helping him surmount obstacles or resistance as they arise and by encouraging him to restructure his daily life around the 12-Step program of Alcoholics Anonymous, Narcotics Anonymous or Gamblers Anonymous, as appropriate.

2. To stimulate and support ongoing personal development by the provision of *Growth Groups* in which both
   dependent and concerned persons can participate.
   Here the focus is on interpersonal communication,
   self-knowledge, exploration of new, adaptive patterns
   of interaction and behavior and initiation and enhance-
   ment of healthy relationships.
3. To offer professional therapy and specialized services
   to individuals, couples and families who require assistance with specific adjustment difficulties.
4. To endorse a support-seeking, mutually-helpful response between aftercare participants so that people
   operate as a resource for each other.

In discussing treatment, we have emphasized the positive benefits that can be gained by both dependent and
concerned persons. With professional guidance and an
attitude of responsibility for self, each participant becomes able to achieve the level of personal growth with
which he or she is comfortable, at that time. Each person
further learns to understand and respond to others so that
relationships deepen.

Change and growth are challenging but difficult. Treatment does not aim to produce happy, problem-free families.
That, of course, is unrealistic. The process and themes of
treatment we have discussed so far encourage the emergence of authentic people – with real needs, real conflicts,
real resources. Participants learn to know themselves and
accept others. Perfection is no longer desired but a positive
attitude to self-development and problem-solving is acquired
with the support of others. Enhanced personal identity,
within the context of a shared life, is, for many a valued
achievement of this period. Self-respect, recognition of
choice and acceptance of responsibility for their direction
in life characterized participants who have done well in a
program. At its best, then, treatment offers a new beginning.
Recovery is the base from which individuals and families
develop potential and respond effectively to changing circumstances as their lives unfold.

When recovery is established and normality restored, most dependent and concerned persons deeply appreciate the gains they have made. Their lives are richer, their self-respect higher than ever before. They have learned to like themselves and each other and to value the bonds they established while working through the pain of dependency.

11

Surprise Ending

Before Annette came in to treatment, I really felt our relationship was over. I just didn't want to be with her anymore. She had changed beyond recognition. She took so many pills and drank secretly. She slept most of the day. Our children were really frightened of her. She was irritable and unfair with them and I'm pretty sure she punished them too much. I couldn't take her anywhere. She was always drunk, falling around. That wasn't the worst thing, though. She'd become so aggressive, insulting people; being really sarcastic and nasty with me. She often tried to make me jealous by flirting with other men. She was just messy, though. Everyone was embarrassed for her though I don't believe she realized that. She thought she was the life and soul of the party. It was pathetic.

I couldn't help feeling ashamed. She stopped washing and looking nice. I just couldn't bear to sleep with her anymore. I had no interest whatsoever. In my line of work, I got lots of offers — attractive girls, fun to be with, no hassle . . . It was tempting. I couldn't help comparing them with Annette. She didn't just come out second — she came out last. I wouldn't have minded so much for myself but the kids. I just wasn't happy to have them live like that. I earned enough. I reckoned I could manage without Annette.

My mother offered to help; she's really great with them. They love her. I thought it would be okay. I had my mind made up, really, before treatment. But I felt I owed Annette a chance to get herself sorted out — so I stood by her while she was in the program.

I must say, I found it hard. I didn't really want to go back over all those incidents in the past. I sort of wanted to blot them out of my mind. Still, the lectures were interesting and the counselors really knew their business. They could get through . . . you know? I suppose, in spite of myself, I started getting involved. One of the things that really astounded me was the similarity between us all. I mean, Annette thought, acted and felt exactly the same as everyone else in treatment. I had the same ideas and feelings as other husbands and some of the wives too. It was a revelation really. Up to then, I always thought Annette's problems were just something that had happened in our family. I never thought of it as an illness — a dependency. In spite of myself, I found I began to learn and put pieces together. All those symptoms, the person-ality change, manipulation, amnesia, disinhibited behavior — typ-ical, every one of them.

About halfway through, I was beginning to feel — "Well, at least I now understand what was wrong. I can see she's not a bad or lazy person. Besides, she really does seem to be trying hard. Her counselors are pleased and physically she looks better than she has in years." Then, I remember one day I was there to take part in group therapy. Annette looked dreadful. Her eyes were red with weeping and she hadn't bothered with her hair. My heart dropped when I saw her. I thought, "Oh, no. She's gone back. She stopped progressing!" I was amazed I was so disappointed. I really felt devastated. I also was angry with her, until I understood.

The day before, Annette's counselor had telephoned to ask if I could arrange to bring the children to the treatment center — just for a while during the day. They were with me when I came and my mother was planning to pick them up in about an hour.

I don't think I'll ever forget Annette's face when she looked at them. I had one arm around our daughter and the other around our son as she turned toward us. She looked . . . haunted! Tears streamed silently down her face and she clenched and unclenched her fists, twisting and knotting her handkerchief. At first, I thought she would run over, then she seemed to check herself and just stood there, her face turned away, her eyes glistening. I couldn't stop looking at her. I still didn't understand. How could she frighten the children like this? How could she let them see her in this state?

It was Mark, our son, who broke the tension. Suddenly he was running — running toward her! "Mom, Mom, don't cry. We love you." He literally threw himself at her, grabbed her and held on as hard as he could. Mandy streaked after him. They were all crying and hugging and Annette kept touching them tentatively, whispering, "I'm sorry — so sorry I hurt you."

At last I understood. Annette had begun to realize how her dependency affected us. Her defenses were down. She was overwhelmed with guilt and felt unworthy — unsure how we would receive her. I felt as though ice was melting inside my chest. My eyes filled up. I could hardly see them, through a blur of tears — my family, my wife.

I wanted to cry and cry but didn't know how. I hardly noticed the hand on my shoulder. I could scarcely see Joe, Annette's counselor, standing beside me. "She's getting well," he said, "but she needs a little more help. I think we should all talk together. Would you like to?" Numbly, I nodded and we went to Joe's office. I felt awkward with Annette and avoided looking at her, though my heart was full of feeling for her.

I still can't remember exactly what was said during that session. Joe was wonderful. He was able to help the children understand what was wrong with their mom in a way I couldn't. I thought they'd be frightened but they weren't — not at all. They just wanted to know if Mom would get better now. Joe explained to them what Annette would need to do, how she couldn't drink or take pills and would have to go to meetings to help her. The kids thought it was kind of like having to go to school — they were astounding. They were so loving but they also told Annette how frightened they'd been and how strangely she used to look sometimes. Mandy, who's only seven, asked if Mom would be awake more now during the day. She told Annette how scary it was to come home from school and find her sleeping. Annette cried and laughed and listened. I believe she was really hearing the children for the first time in years. I suppose I heard some things I didn't know, too. I realized I'd been so full of anger with Annette and contempt for her that I had never really tried to understand compulsion or to imagine what it felt like for her in that twilight drug-induced haze. She was lonely and guilty and full of remorse. It was so sad . . . I had been so distant from her, ready to abandon her to pills and booze. Now I felt bad.

I could feel the tears come as I spoke about it. How I hadn't really understood and how angry I'd been . . . Joe comforted me and listened. Then he said, "Annette's begun to realize what her dependency cost . . . all those lost years . . . the hurt . . . the distance . . . She's at a point of choice now. Annette, you can go back to a chemically-dominated world or you can recover and live normally. Whether you'll live with your family depends, I think, on the progress you make. It's a decision you and your husband will have to make together. At the moment, why don't we just wait and see how things work out."

That's how we left it for then. After that I found I looked foward to seeing Annette. I made a point of attending all the program requirements for concerned persons. I really started listening and learning.

I identified more than I believed possible and I never before felt so comfortable with people. They really understood and I could talk about myself and listen to them as well. I began to see how we'd all been affected, how our emotions had become bottled up . . . I really worked on myself. I didn't feel angry anymore and could be warm and natural with Annette. We could even laugh together, just like the old days!

My mother and I visited together one day. She couldn't believe the difference she saw in Annette. She was peaceful and nondefensive. She thanked my mom for her kindness toward the children over the years. She talked freely about her dependency and didn't try to hide anything. She said she'd really have to work hard to stay sober but she hoped she would.

"I want it more than anything else," she said, "I'll destroy myself if I use alcohol or pills again."

Mom and I talked about it going home in the car. We were both impressed and felt Annette was really serious about sobriety. Mom is one of the most tactful people I know and would never embarrass me by asking a direct question. This time she didn't need to ask. I knew what was on her mind. It was on mine, too. Would Annette be coming home to us? I was silent for a long time, thinking it out. Aloud, I murmured, "I'll talk to Joe, Annette's counselor. We'll see what he thinks."

Well, Joe and I talked and Annette and Joe and I talked and we agreed. Annette would come home because she and I both wanted it. Naturally, of course, so did the children. However, our agreement was clear. Annette belonged at home as long as she was in recovery and sober. If she stopped working her program or relapsed, we'd have to rethink.

That was two years ago. Annette and the children and I are together and happy. In fact, I believe we're closer than we ever were. She looks wonderful these days. There's a new serenity about her and she lives in the present — one day at a time. So do I. It's a great philosophy of life.

Still, it wasn't all easy. We had some pretty bad times after intensive treatment finished. There were communication failures, moodiness (on my part, too, I'll admit). I suppose we had to get to know each other again. We really needed our aftercare program and our self-support groups. They helped us through plenty of tough spots. In spite of the hard times, I'm grateful we had the chance. It's a new life now, better, richer than before. It's odd, when Annette was active and drunk or drugged all the time, I often thought, "If only we could get back to normal." It's funny; that seems so strange to me now . . . There's no going back. We've all changed and grown — but at last we've got the normality bit right.

References

It is impossible to write about dependency, enabling and intervention without being influenced by the work and concepts of others. While material from other sources was not used directly in the preparation of the book I wish to acknowledge indebtedness to the Hazelden Publications and to the following books.

Bratton, Mary, **A Guide To Family Intervention.** Pompano Beach, Florida: Health Communications, 1987.

Cruse, Joseph R., **Painful Affairs: Looking For Love Through Addiction And Co-dependency.** Deerfield Beach, Florida: Health Communications, 1989.

Drews, Toby Rice, **Getting Them Sober,** Volume 1. South Plainfield, New Jersey: Bridge Publishing, 1980.

Fajardo, Roque, **Helping Your Alcoholic *Before* He Or She Hits Bottom.** New York: Crown Publishers, 1976.

Gold, Mark S., M.D., **800-COCAINE.** New York: Bantam Books, 1984.

Johnson, Vernon E., **I'll Quit Tomorrow.** San Francisco, California: Harper and Row, 1980.

Kellerman, Joseph L., **Alcoholism: A Merry-Go-Round Called Denial.** Pamphlet. Center City, Minnesota: Hazelden, 1980.

Kellerman, Joseph L., **A Guide for the Family of an Alcholic.** Pamphlet. Center City Minnesota: Hazelden, 1980.

Meagher, M. David, **Beginning of A Miracle: How to Intervene with the Alcoholic or Addicted Person.** Pompano Beach, Florida: Health Communications, 1987.

Milam, James R. and Katherine Ketchum, **Under the Influence.** Seattle, Washington: Madrona Publishers, 1981.

Wegscheider, Sharon, **Another Chance: Hope and Health for Alcholic Families.** Palo Alto, California: Science and Behavior Books, Inc., 1980.

Other Books By . . .
Health Communications, Inc.

ADULT CHILDREN OF ALCOHOLICS
Janet Woititz
Over a year on *The New York Times* Best Seller list, this book is the primer on Adult Children of Alcoholics.
ISBN 0-932194-15-X $6.95

STRUGGLE FOR INTIMACY
Janet Woititz
Another best-seller, this book gives insightful advice on learning to love more fully.
ISBN 0-932194-25-7 $6.95

DAILY AFFIRMATIONS: For Adult Children of Alcoholics
Rokelle Lerner
These positive affirmations for every day of the year paint a mental picture of your life as you choose it to be.
ISBN 0-932194-27-3 $6.95

CHOICEMAKING: For Co-dependents, Adult Children and Spirituality Seekers — Sharon Wegscheider-Cruse
This useful book defines the problems and solves them in a positive way.
ISBN 0-932194-26-5 $9.95

LEARNING TO LOVE YOURSELF: Finding Your Self-Worth
Sharon Wegscheider-Cruse
"Self-worth is a choice, not a birthright", says the author as she shows us how we can choose positive self-esteem.
ISBN 0-932194-39-7 $7.95

BRADSHAW ON: THE FAMILY: A Revolutionary Way of Self-Discovery
John Bradshaw
The host of the nationally televised series of the same name shows us how families can be healed and individuals can realize full potential.
ISBN 0-932194-54-0 $9.95

HEALING THE CHILD WITHIN:
Discovery and Recovery for Adult Children of Dysfunctional Families
Charles Whitfield
Dr. Whitfield defines, describes and discovers how we can reach our Child Within to heal and nurture our woundedness.
ISBN 0-932194-40-0 $8.95

Enterprise Center, 3201 S.W. 15th Street,
Deerfield Beach, FL 33442
1-800-851-9100

Health Communications, Inc.